PRAISE FOR *WINNING CUSTOMER CENTRICITY*

"Despite my trying to practice it e   *Customer Centricity* still provided me with   king, and much needed discipline that I will take back to work. A must-read for today's and tomorrow's marketeers."

Paul Polman, CEO Unilever

"Putting the customer first has been, is and will remain the whole focus of marketing for many decades. What seems like a simple, "good common sense" idea is so hard to put into meaningful actions that many companies continue to struggle with the execution of customer focus. In *Winning Customer Centricity*, Denyse Drummond-Dunn provides hands-on recommendations on how to implement a successful customer strategy execution within 50 weeks! It works; her advice will do wonders for your company and your clients!"

Prof. Dominique Turpin, President IMD

"Can you answer this one simple question? Who are our customers and how do they buy? If your answer is no, *Winning Customer Centricity* is for you; and even if you think that you know your customers, this book will give you some personal epiphanies on your journey to truly knowing who your customers are."

Martyn Etherington, CMO Mitel, author of Diary of a CMO

"Most companies want to be customer centric, but in reality, few are. Denyse lays our the core foundational elements needed from organizational design to company culture to instill customer centricity at the heart of an organization. This is a must read for organizations ready and willing to put their customer needs at the core of business decisions."

David Armano, Global Strategy Director Edelman Digital

Winning Customer Centricity

Putting Customers at the Heart of
Your Business—One Day at a Time

Denyse Drummond-Dunn

Visit us on our website, http://www.C3Centricity.com, and sign up for our blog posts. You will get access to all the latest videos, articles and thoughts on customer centricity from around the globe. Or sign up for free to the C³C Members area too and get even more.

E-Mail: Info@C3Centricity.com

ISBN: 978-2-9700998-0-2 (sc)
ISBN: 978-2-9700998-1-9 (hc)
ISBN: 978-2-9700998-2-6 (e)

Library of Congress Control Number: 2014916508

Published by C³Centricity, 2/25/2015

This book is dedicated to everyone I have ever met – the good, the bad, and the crazy. You may have inspired me, excited me, challenged or frustrated me, but together you have made me who I am today.
Thank you.

Contents

Introduction to Processes 89

Acknowledgements

This book has been made possible by the support and ideas of many people.

In particular, I would like to thank Christian Moreillon of BrozerMo in Savigny, near Lausanne, Switzerland, for designing the great cover page as well as creating the layout template that has breathed life into my words.

Heartfelt thanks are also due to my many proof-readers who offered constructive criticism during this book's writing and especially at the editing stage. These included Marianne Bollaert-Bassil, David Dolezel, Gavin Dickinson, Jana Fabianova, Juan Felix, Michael Gentle, Giovanni Giro, Alan Hill, Oksana Klepova, Olga Kornilova, Christophe Mayca, Andrew Reid, Julia Sedenkova, and Ivor Shalofsky. Forgive me if I have forgotten anyone.

Finally a special word of thanks to Jody Moxham and Terry Villines, who supported me through the challenge of writing the book and then defining, selecting, and improving the illustrations.

Introduction

> **❝** *To be successful, you have to have your heart in your business and your business in your heart*
>
> **Thomas John Watson Sr,** American chairman and former CEO of IBM

Let me start by introducing you to your customers. That is how we will refer to them here, but depending upon the industry in which you work, your organisation may prefer to call them *consumers* or *clients*. Whatever name you use, these are arguably the most important people to your business. Why? Because they are the ones who spend their hard-earned cash on your products and services. They make your business viable and hopefully also profitable.

Customer centricity is an essential part of doing business today and ensures growth for all people-facing industries, both now and in the future. Making an organisation more customer centric takes full commitment from every single employee, as everyone has a role to play in satisfying and hopefully delighting the customer.

This book is intended to accompany you on your journey to winning customer centricity and is divided into fifty weeks of actions to take - that leaves you two weeks for vacation! Some steps are small and easy to complete. Others may take more than a week to accomplish but can at least be started in the week under review.

Each section ends with a summary of what you should have achieved and the things that may have already changed within your organisation as a result. If you would like to compare your successes and future opportunities for change with others on the same journey, join the discussion in the members' area of the C³Centricity website at http://www.C3Centricity.com/C3CMembers.

In the members section of the website, you'll also find many free templates which will be an invaluable resource for you in tracking your progress and comparing results. As you read each week and follow the examples given, you will undoubtedly have ideas of further actions to take, or maybe some that you are not ready to undertake for the moment but would like to capture for development at a later stage. Use the section notes templates to capture them. These notes will also be a precious support in the final week, when you go back over your year to plan for the coming twelve months and the new actions to be undertaken.

This book is designed to enable you to review all areas of your business over the next twelve months. The suggested steps and actions are divided into four essential areas: the customer, the company, the products and services you offer, and the processes you use internally. Ideally, it would make sense to go through the book in the order proposed, as some actions build upon those of previous weeks. However, if you know your main area of weakness, you can jump first to that section before going back and reviewing the other recommended actions.

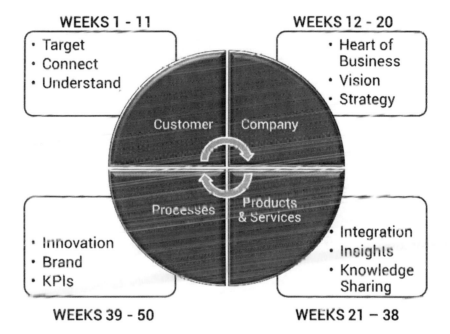

If you're not sure where your greatest opportunity lies at present, complete the online C³C Evaluator tool. It's also available in the members' area at http://www.C3Centricity.com/C3CMembers.

Although this book is designed as a year in review, you can of course take a longer or shorter time to follow through on all the suggested actions mentioned. You may even decide to make this book a permanent reference guide, followed from year to year, to optimise your customer centricity in an on-going fashion. The choice is yours.

Reading this book should provide you with the inspiration you have always searched for to support needed change in your customer centricity. If you would like assistance during the year on any of the topics covered in this book, please let me know. I would love to support your success.

Finally, I welcome questions and feedback. If you have any comments or concerns that have not been addressed here or in the members' area, please contact me at Denysedd@C3Centricity.com. I look forward to hearing from you.

Introduction to the Customer

Over the next eleven weeks, you will review what you need to know about your customers – how to target the right ones, how to connect with them, and how to understand their needs in order to satisfy them completely.

Week 1: Show you Care

Objective

This is your first step towards customer-centric excellence: to show you really care about your customer. This week, think about the above quote and what it really means to the business you are in. Do all members of the organisation understand that it is the customer who pays their wages and that without customers they wouldn't have a job?

Action

Share the above quote with everyone in the company. Put it at the beginning of every presentation you give, and add it – or perhaps your own preferred quote about the customer – to your signature on emails. You can find further quotes about the customer at http://www.C3Centricity.com/Library.

Ensure everyone understands why change is necessary, and find ways to demonstrate clearly that every employee, from the executive board down, visibly supports this priority company objective.

Examples

Prove you're serious about becoming more customer centric by signing all your emails with a suitable quote or a challenging question. For example:

- Always remember: "*There may be customers without brands, but there are no brands without customers*" (Anonymous)
- Ask yourself: What have you done for your customer today?
- Always remember: "*We don't pay your wages, our customers do, every time they buy our products/services.*" (Adapted from Henry Ford)
- Ask yourself: Did you find new ways to satisfy our customers today?

Idea

Further thoughts to get you going:

- Start every meeting and presentation with a picture of a real customer.
- Put photos of your customers on every floor of the building, especially where employees gather, such as a coffee area or canteen/restaurant.
- Decorate lift doors and hallways with pictures of customers.
- End every meeting by asking "*What would our customers think of the decision we have just taken?*"

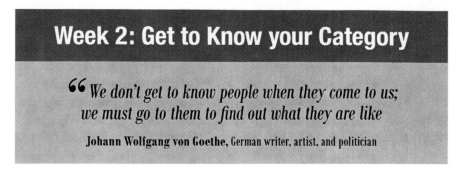

66 *We don't get to know people when they come to us; we must go to them to find out what they are like*

Johann Wolfgang von Goethe, German writer, artist, and politician

Objective

Identify the exact category of products or services in which your brand is participating and get to know its consumers/users and shoppers.

Action

Review everything you know about those involved in your category – the people who choose, buy, consume, write, tweet, or post about the products or services. What do you know about them? What are their similarities and differences?

Examples

Thinking of the customer first requires a lot of little changes and everyone's involvement. Here are some examples for getting everyone interested and curious about your customer:

- Start by reviewing all the information you have internally about the category's customers from market research studies, external reports, and employee knowledge. Make a summary and circulate to all departments.
- If people are already curious about customers, provide one document to each person and ask him or her to summarise it with the three points found to be the most important or surprising. Then share and exchange ideas.
- Share stories about your category users from your own experiences or those of your family and friends. Publish the best, most interesting, or most surprising in your company newsletter.
- If you own retail oulets or your product is available in them, spend time watching how the products and services are compared and purchased.

Week 3: Run a Segmentation

Objective

This week, concentrate on how you are choosing the customers you target for each of your brands. Are you just taking anyone who buys in that category, or are you targeting a specific group? The best way to choose a target audience is to run a segmentation of all category users and then identify the group most likely to be interested in your offer.

Action

Your action this week is to initiate a segmentation exercise – or if you already have one, to review the results in preparation for next week's action of choosing the target audience for each of your brands.

A segmentation analysis can be as simple as identifying your users by what you see, such as young men or empty nesters (older parents whose children have left home). Or it can be as complex as targeting people who value freedom and are looking for brands that can fulfil or suggest this dream. This more detailed and complex description would come from a "values and motivation" segmentation.

All good segmentations will fulfil five conditions known collectively as MIDAS.

- *Measurable*: Criteria are clearly defined and quantifiable, such as size, market share, and value share.
- *Identifiable*: Each segment has a distinct profile, and each customer can be assigned to only one.
- *Definable*: The segmentation is easy to describe and share with others.
- *Actionable*: It's easy to identify and target your actions based on the segmentation.
- *Substantial*: The segmentation is financially viable, stable, or growing, and durable in the long term.

Review your segmentation and decide how it can be improved, whether by completing the information on each group or by running a whole new study. It is definitely worth having a solid and actionable segmentation of category users, as this will form the very foundation of your brand's customer centricity.

Examples

The graph below from Econsultancy shows the usage of different types of segmentation. The results clearly show that the more complex a segmentation is, the more competitive it will be, because fewer organisations are using it.

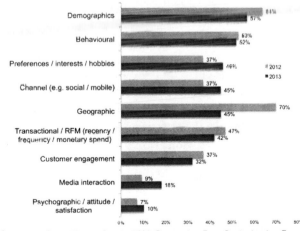

Source: RedEye / Econsultancy 2013 Conversion Rate Optimization Report,
https://econsultancy.com/reports/conversion-rate-optimization-report-2013

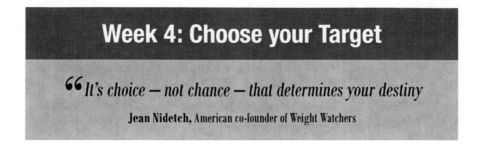

Objective

If you have a recent segmentation study with which you are comfortable, take this extra week to review and refine your choice of target audience. If you don't have the money, time, or expertise to run a segmentation study as suggested last week, you can still make an informed decision about your target group by using simple criteria that can be observed or obtained from basic market research studies.

Action

Identify a number of criteria by which you can group your potential customers and then use a matrix, such as the simplified example opposite (developed by BCG in the 90s and enhanced by GE and McKinsey) to input whatever information you have. Whilst the criteria you use for each axis may vary, you can complete them over time, so don't worry if at first you are only using a few pieces of data for each axis, such as segment size, category development, fit to your brand, product attractiveness, distribution, or media usage.

Once you have positioned your different segments or groups of users, you can easily see which one is your primary target and then what needs to be done for each of the others as a second priority. Consider the following possibilities:

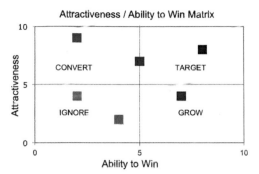

Attractiveness / Ability to Win Matrix

- *Target:* your primary customers. You probably have many of them, so your action will be to maintain their interest and protect them from competition.
- *Convert:* users who are attracted to your product or service but you haven't been able to win over. Look more closely at their particular desires and consider what you can do to better appeal to them.
- *Grow:* your product or service can easily win these customers, but perhaps they are not as profitable as you would like. Review your products from time to time and develop strategies to make them more attractive.
- *Ignore:* many organisations struggle to disregard some category users, but if you have neither the right product nor segment profitability, why spend time and energy going after them?

Examples

All successful brands have identified a target audience to attract and satisfy. Here are examples from some of the major consumer goods companies:

- Kit Kat Chunky was developed to be a new chocolate biscuit snack more appealing to younger men.
- Marlboro cigarettes were relaunched to appeal to those sensitive to the values of freedom and independence. The original target audience for the brand was actually female smokers, as it had a red tip!
- Coca-Cola Light was first developed to appeal to female carbonated-soft-drink consumers who were careful about the calories they absorbed.

Idea

Have some fun by trying to identify the target for brands you see advertised. This can also be an enjoyable team activity or precursor to segmentation work, and helps everyone understand its importance.

Week 5: Describe your Customers

❝ *The more you engage with customers, the clearer things become and the easier it is to determine what you should be doing*

John Russell, British chairman of WMMC, former CEO of Manganese Bronze, former VP of Harley Davidson Europe

Objective

Last week you spent time identifying the differences between the customers for each of your brands and choosing the specific audience for each one. Now take a look at the descriptions you have made for each and complete them with as much detail as you can.

Action

Complete a detailed description of the customers for each of your brands, including:

- *Who:* their major demographics, including gender, age, geography, and socioeconomic class.
- *What:* what they buy, consume, or do when purchasing or using the product or service.
- *Where:* the location where people consume, purchase, read about, see displayed, or receive communication about the product or service.

- *Why:* the reasons behind their purchase, consumption, use, reading about, or shopping for the product or service.

The deeper you go into the description of your customers, the better your understanding of them will be and the more difficult it will be for a competitor to steal them.

One last point to keep in mind: People today are changing more rapidly than ever before, so it's important to continually review and update your description of your customers with the latest information and knowledge about them. The same information should also be collected about your major competitors.

Examples

The 4W™ template is an example of what should be included in your customer description. The more information you include from different sources, the more deeply you will understand your customers and the more likely you will be to satisfy and delight them. You can download the template from the C³Centricity site at http://www.C3Centricity.com/C3CMembers.

Template		Chocolate Bar	
WHO	WHAT	WHO	WHAT
Demographics Life-stage Lifestyle	Use/Consume Purchase Read Listen Watch Surf	Men 25-35yo Single Lives in City Rents apartment Plays team sports	Single chocolate bars Buy chocolate weekly Read TimeOut Listen to FM radio Tweets regularly Uses FourSquare to find friends
WHERE	WHY	WHERE	WHY
Use/Consume Buy Read Listen Watch Surf	Needs Preferences Attitudes Emotions Motivations	Buys chocolate bar in kiosk Eats chocolate after sports match Listens to radio in car Meets friends after sports for a drink	Eats chocolate as no time for a meal Prefers single bars as they offer more choice Thinks brand ABC is for men not wmen Thick chocolate is satisfying Nuts are filling

Idea

Always keep your customer profile template or description close to you whilst you work. Update it whenever you learn something new, whether from observation, market research or other sources.

Week 6: Evaluate Customer Value

> ❝ The only value your company will ever create, is the value that comes from customers — the ones you have now and the ones you will have in the future

> **Don Peppers and Martha Rogers,** American co-founders of Peppers & Rogers Group, and co-authors of six books

Objective

You have now chosen and defined who the target audience is for each of your brands and completed a detailed description of these customers. This week, you need to review their value to the business – in other words, what they will be worth over their lifetime to the organisation. This will help you further refine who your target audience is by allowing you to eliminate those customers who have a lower return on your future investments.

Action

For each of your brands, calculate the target audience's lifetime value. The simplest way to do this is with an equation:

$$\frac{\text{Annual Revenue} \times \text{Margin} \times \text{Years}}{\text{Churn Rate (attrition, switching)}}$$

If you have segmented your category users into several groups or clusters, this calculation can be done for each segment separately. This has the advantage of helping you prioritise the groups in terms of their value to the overall business and also serves as verification that you have made the right choice of target audience.

Examples

There are far more sophisticated ways to calculate customer lifetime value than the simple equation given above. Each formula may contain some or all of the following elements in its calculation:

- number of customers you have
- average spend per purchase
- average number of purchases per year
- yearly customer churn (percentage of customers that do not buy in a given period, for example in the past twelve months)
- retention rate (100 – churn rate)
- cost of customer acquisition (costs associated with getting a customer to buy, including market research, marketing, and advertising)
- discount rate (often ignored, but the most accurate calculations include this number, which captures the cost of future discounts to retain the customer, such as promotions and customer support)
- customer lifetime period (number of periods, usually years, in the life of a customer; five to ten years is usually used, since a longer period is seen as being too unreliable)

Choose the most relevant elements to calculate your brand's own lifetime value based upon the category and information availability.

Idea

If you have never done a lifetime value calculation before, the simple equation above is a good place to start. As your needs and understanding grow, you can start to incorporate more complex elements and calculations as relevant from the above list.

Week 7: Connect with your Customers

Objective

This week, you'll identify the best way to connect with the people you have identified and described, in order to understand them even better. If you have a largely completed profile, then you should know all your customers' habits, including their leisure activities and their media and shopping habits. This should help you to easily find your customers, as it is time to get closer to them.

Action

Make use of all the opportunities you have to connect with your target customers in order to further deepen your knowledge and understanding of them. Every employee should spend half a day (at least) this week in some form of customer connection.

Examples

Most, if not all, customer-facing organisations have several forms of direct contact with their customers, including the following:

- retail/advisory outlets
- promotions, demonstrations and sampling activities
- call centre/care centre
- website or online social media platforms

All of these provide opportunities to get closer to your customers.

Idea

If there is a market research project being conducted this week, ask your colleagues in your market research and insight group to arrange for you to accompany an interviewer or attend a focus group, in-depth interview, observation, or ethnographic exercise.

Week 8: Share your Experiences

> **❝ If you use standard research methods, you will have the same insights as everyone else**
>
> **David Nichols,** author and managing partner at The Brandgym

Objective

Last week you connected with your target customer, perhaps for the very first time. Did you connect during a market research study, at an event, by listening in on their calls into your call centre, or perhaps by reading their tweets or comments online? Whichever way you connected, I bet it was exciting!

Your understanding of your customers increases this week with another connection – this time, using a different channel. If you listened in to your call centre, why not go out and meet your customers in retail outlets?

Action

Organise another customer connection event for all employees, but this time, follow up immediately afterwards with a sharing session. Try a "lunch and learn" event or an aperitif to make the occasion more convivial. You can all learn so much from each other's encounters, and sharing enables everyone to compare and contrast their experiences. This multiplies the impact of the learning for everyone and already starts the process of information integration with other knowledge held internally. In addition, it prepares the ground for the identification of possible future opportunities and challenges.

Examples

The main objective of building your customer understanding, by sharing and integrating all you have learnt, can be achieved in many ways. Here are a few examples to get you started:

- Hold monthly "lunch and learn" sessions in a relaxed, fun, and creative environment. Share all the latest market research results, connection findings, or care centre topics that customers have called in about.
- Publish the latest themes customers are calling, writing, or tweeting about. Put it somewhere visible to stimulate everyone's thinking. How about posting weekly summaries on the notice board, at the lift, in the restaurant waiting area, at the water fountain, or anywhere else in your office where a maximum number of people can be inspired by the information?
- Add an item to everyone's annual objectives in which they must conduct a certain number of contacts with customers each year, or at a certain frequency.

Although most employees have now connected in two different ways with your customers, this should become an on-going exercise so that everyone in the organisation remains current about changes in your customers' attitudes and behaviours.

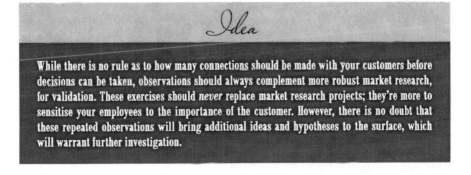

Idea

While there is no rule as to how many connections should be made with your customers before decisions can be taken, observations should always complement more robust market research, for validation. These exercises should *never* replace market research projects; they're more to sensitise your employees to the importance of the customer. However, there is no doubt that these repeated observations will bring additional ideas and hypotheses to the surface, which will warrant further investigation.

Week 9: Involve Your Customers

Objective

Over the last two weeks, you have been connecting with, listening to, and watching your target audience. Now it's time to become a little more intimate with them by having an actual conversation about a topic of interest.

Action

Identify opportunities to discuss topics with or ask questions of your customers. This will show customers that you are interested in them and appreciate their feedback, ideas, and criticisms. These connections can be made through online media, at the end of calls into your call/care centre, at the completion of a market research questionnaire, or in a separate study – such as during in-depth interviews or focus-group discussions.

Look for topics of which you would like to have a better understanding, or on which you believe your customers' input could be of use. For example, ask for opinions on a new aroma, flavour, or product concept. Internet sessions are of great value to regional or global organisations, since they provide every employee with the opportunity to observe, read, or even participate in the exchanges.

Customers are particularly enthusiastic about innovation or creative sessions, often called *co-creation sessions,* as such events provide them with feelings of pride and importance. These are strong emotions that will almost certainly prompt them to share their experience with friends and family afterwards, if not to a much wider audience online. What a great boost to your brand's image!

Management may feel uncomfortable about sharing creative and new-product concepts with people outside of the organisation. This can be addressed by:

- Choosing people within your own organisation who are not directly involved in the area, such as factory workers or those working in a different business unit, who are category users.
- Ensuring that your MR supplier carefully scrutinizes each participant for potential confidentiality issues and makes each one sign a nondisclosure document.

Although neither of these will guarantee total discretion and confidentiality, any possible risks will be minimised. If management is really against external testing, just accept that you can only work with employees within the group and acknowledge the possibility of introducing biases, such as extreme positivity or above-average category awareness and knowledge.

Examples

Many organisations are already contacting their customers on a regular basis to help them in their decision-making. For example, Nespresso connects with their Le Club members to gather opinions about new blends or feedback on their latest advertising campaign. Both Unilever and Nestlé use online groups to discuss advertising, promotions, or new product ideas with their customers.

Procter & Gamble, one of the first companies to involve their customers, have developed these connections into what has become known as Tremor™ in the United States. (http://www.tremor.com.)

Imagine what your company could learn from that kind of connectedness!

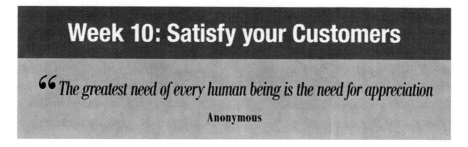

Objective

Now that you know your customers really well, your task this week is to identify how you are going to better satisfy them, using Maslow's hierachy of needs for inspiration.

Action

According to the generally accepted understanding of Maslow's theory, human beings are motivated by unsatisfied needs, and there is a specific order to meeting these needs that must be respected. The lower ones, such as physiological and safety needs, must be satisfied before higher requirements can be addressed.

If you are looking to sell in developing markets, where people are still concerned about personal safety, brands positioned *only* on needs of status and self-actualization are unlikely to succeed. It may be viable for a niche positioning, but you cannot go after a mass market with such a self-limiting positioning.

While it may be true that customers in emerging markets today are attracted to expensive products, adaptations will be needed to make those products viable at market level (e.g. premium shampoo sold in sachets rather than bottles).

Identify the need you are most likely addressing with each of your brands or services, based upon the detailed description of your target customers. You can do this by identifying what motivates them to use the category and which need is as yet insufficiently or not at all fulfilled, to which your offer could respond.

Examples

Several companies have already been inspired by Maslow's hierarchy of needs, especially in their communications, including the following:

- Axe uses its communication to position itself at the middle, psychological need of intimate relationships, especially aimed at the young. Axe (known as Lynx in the UK) suggests that its products make their users irresistibly attractive to the opposite sex.
- Marlboro's cowboy is still associated with the brand even today, despite cigarette advertising having been banned in many markets. He is perceived as manly, strong, powerful, and tough – but also as kind, hard working, and determined. The cowboy stands for moral behaviour and friendship, rather than family, since he is also seen as somewhat of a loner.

  Interestingly, in those markets where advertising has been banned and where the "gold" or "light" products are the more popular versions, Marlboro has been able to reposition itself on the pyramid and now responds more to needs of self-esteem. The one need linking these two positions is confidence, which explains Marlboro's continued success even after this repositioning.
- Cartier's "Odyssée" film is an exceptionally long advertisement that was first aired in 2012. It is aiming to appeal to people looking for passion and creativity, those at the top of Maslow's hierarchy.

Idea

In recent years, there has been much debate about Maslow's needs being a hierarchy. In fact, Maslow did not present them as a pyramid; this developed over the years as his theory was supported and adapted by users. Whether or not you agree with the hierarchy, the identification of the needs you are addressing is still a valuable exercise to complete.

> **66** *All human actions have one or more of these seven causes:*
> *chance, nature, compulsions, habit, reason, passion, desire*
>
> **Aristotle,** Greek philosopher and polymath, student of Plato, teacher of Alexander the Great

Objective

By now you are probably more than two months into your journey to improved customer centricity and have identified who your target customers are and how to connect with and satisfy them. In order to persuade them to purchase your product or service, you need to find a way to communicate that resonates with them and their unfulfilled needs. We'll identify that message this week.

Action

Review the completed description of your target customers and the identified level of Maslow's hierarchy of needs they are on when using your product or service category. Brands that are positioned to address relevant needs will better resonate and make your communications more motivating.

Review your campaign plan and ensure that you are clearly addressing relevant needs. If this is not the case, consider working on a new advertising concept and promotional plan to better focus on them. Such an approach will almost certainly resonate more effectively with your customers, although this should of course be verified before implementation.

Examples

Since Maslow's hierarchy has been in use for a long time, especially in the development of communications, there are numerous examples of brands which have successfully addressed their target customers' needs. All three brands mentioned last week have advertising that communicates clear associations with the unmet needs of their customers.

Another interesting observation is that there can be several different brands that are being positioned on the exact same need, though when in the same category, this is rarely successful. For example, all parents want their children to be able to satisfy their natural curiosity and to grow up happy and healthy. This has recently been used by the following brands:

- Unilever's Omo (Persil/Skip/Via) shows that a good mother lets her child experiment and learn – even if this means getting dirty. See an example from their "Dirt is good" campaign on YouTube at https://m. youtube.com/watch?v LOKdei9modU
- Nestlé's Nido portrays this need by showing a mother providing the nourishment for healthy growth, which allows her children to explore the outside world safely. If you would like to see an example from their "Let them grow, let them go" campaign from a few years ago, you can check it out on YouTube at http://youtu.be/v8gdyTRJbPA
- Interestingly, Nestlé has illustrated this same need in the advertising for both its bottled water in Asia and its Purina Pet Care in the Americas.

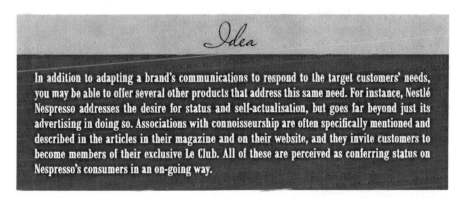

Idea

In addition to adapting a brand's communications to respond to the target customers' needs, you may be able to offer several other products that address this same need. For instance, Nestlé Nespresso addresses the desire for status and self-actualisation, but goes far beyond just its advertising in doing so. Associations with connoisseurship are often specifically mentioned and described in the articles in their magazine and on their website, and they invite customers to become members of their exclusive Le Club. All of these are perceived as conferring status on Nespresso's consumers in an on-going way.

Your Summary Results for the Customer Section

Over the past eleven weeks, you have spent a lot of time thinking about your customers. Look at the table below and ensure that you have completed each of the recommended actions in each of the eleven areas. If you would like to, you can download a copy of the template at http://www.C3Centricity.com/C3CMembers and mark whether or not each area has been completed.

Week	Result	Completed? (Y / N)
1	Do you show you care about your customers openly, every day?	
2	Have you clearly identified your category users?	
3	Do you work with a revised segmentation of category users?	
4	Are you confident that you have chosen the best group of customers for your brand?	
5	Are you comfortable that you know your customers really well from the completion of a detailed (4W™) description of them?	
6	Do you know the lifetime value of your customers?	
7	Have you connected directly with some of your customers?	

Week	Result	Completed? (Y / N)
8	Do you regularly exchange knowledge and experiences of connecting with your customers with other employees?	
9	Have you invited some customers to your meetings and listened to their suggestions and ideas?	
10	Do you clearly understand which of your customers' needs your brand is satisfying?	
11	Do your campaigns now resonate better with your customers as a result of your improved knowledge of them and their needs?	

Completing a copy of the above template will make it easier for you to plan for further improvements when you next return to this section.

Introduction to the Company

For the next nine weeks, you will be looking at all the ways you can put the customer at the heart of your business. At the end of this time, whether you decide to change structure and create the position of a CCO (Chief Customer Officer) or not, the customer will be specifically mentioned in your mission and vision statements, as well as in your strategies.

> **❝** *The structure will automatically provide the pattern for the action which follows*
>
> **Donald Curtis,** American author

Objective

You now know who your customers are and how to satisfy them. This week, we need to start working on the changes that are needed within your company to support the move to a more customer-centric organisation.

Action

In most companies, looking after the customer is seen as the responsibility of marketing, sales, consumer services, or call centre personnel. In a customer-centric business, it becomes everyone's responsibility.

Ensure that each employee has regular customer connections as an annual objective, as well as a way to share what has been learned. To help employees think of the customer first, the customer has to become visible in their daily working lives. Be creative in finding ways to make the customer more present in your offices and in your reports and presentations.

Examples

Thinking customer-first can be achieved by constantly reminding employees that it is the customer who actually pays their wages and is the reason they have a job. Below are some examples of how this can be achieved; pick a couple to get started.

- Start every plan, process, decision, and meeting from the customer's perspective.
- Share a detailed description of the customer so everyone has it in mind as they work on their ideas.
- Put pictures of your target customers in the reception area, together with descriptions and relevant quotes.
- Decorate lifts and corridors with pictures of customers.
- Start meetings with a picture of a typical customer as the first slide of each presentation.
- Have a weekly summary of care centre calls, or the issues and suggestions that were mentioned by callers, and circulate or post them visibly.

These are just a few examples of what can be done to make everyone aware of the importance of the company's customers. Be creative and offer rewards to employees who come up with other ways to help everyone think customer first.

Idea

Are you using the email signature quotes and messages suggested in Week 1? If not, perhaps you could do it now. If you are already using one of the suggested lines, perhaps it's time to change it, so people who read it will react with some fresh thinking and ideas. You can find lots of great quotes on the C3Centricity website at http://www.C3Centricity.com/Library

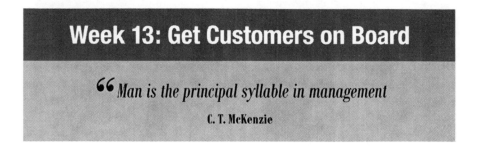

Week 13: Get Customers on Board

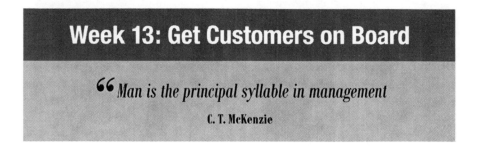

> **❝** *Man is the principal syllable in management*
>
> **C. T. McKenzie**

Objective

Now that you've made the customer visible to everyone in your organisation and everywhere in your offices, it's time to give him or her representation on the executive board.

Action

The best person to represent the customer at the executive level is not the CMO (Chief Marketing Officer), as you might imagine. The CMO is charged with managing brands, and although it is vital that he or she takes the customer into account, the brand should be the CMO's primary focus.

Therefore, someone else should represent the customer, ideally in the created position of chief customer officer or CCO. If this is not possible (for now), make it the CEO's job. He or she already has responsibility for people who are employees and shareholders, so it seems the perfect choice to make the CEO responsible for thinking about the customer too. This will also send a clear message to everyone in the organisation that the customer is not only important but vital to the company.

Another possibility is to give the position to the head of the group that has the most contact with your customers today – namely your vice-president of insight or marketing services.

Examples

One of the most customer-focussed and service-oriented companies today is Zappos. Current CEO Tony Hsieh claims that "customer service shouldn't be a department; it should be the entire company." At Zappos, almost every new hire, including the executives, spends the first month in customer services, including at least two weeks responding to customer calls in the call centre.

How's that for getting really close to the customer? Why not introduce a similar learning experience in your own organisation? If a month is not practical, make it at least a week. After such an experience, it will be almost impossible for employees to forget the customer!

Week 14: Add Customers to your Vision

> **❝**A small group of thoughtful people could change the world. Indeed, it's the only thing that ever has
>
> **Margaret Mead,** American cultural anthropologist, author, and speaker

Objective

Few B2C (Business-to-Consumer) organisations include the customer overtly in their vision and strategy, and yet without customers they would not exist. Make sure you are no longer one of them by reviewing your vision and mission statements this week.

Action

If you are in a people-facing industry, it is vital to start your vision and mission with clear statements that include the fact that your customer is at the heart of your business. A better way to prepare the vision of an organisation is to review the mission statement – what the company is aiming to be – and then to see how this fits in with the target audience that you have now defined and described in detail.

Examples

Some organisations have successfully integrated their customer focus into their mission statement and vision. Here are some examples of the more inspiring ones in my opinion:

- Wells Fargo's vision statement, "We want to satisfy all our customers' financial needs and help them succeed financially."
- Amazon's mission statement, "Our vision is to be earth's most customer centric company; to build a place where people can come to find and discover anything they might want to buy online."
- Ritz-Carlton's credo, "The Ritz-Carlton Hotel is a place where the genuine care and comfort of our guests is our highest mission."
- Google's mission statement, "To organize the world's information and make it universally accessible and useful."
- Apple's mission statement, "To make a contribution to the world by making tools for the mind that advance humankind."

How will you change your own vision and mission statements to include customers more clearly and show the world that they are really at the heart of your business?

Week 15: Prepare for the Future

66 *Strategic planning is worthless —*
unless there is first a strategic vision

John Naisbitt, American author of *Megatrends* and public speaker on futures studies

Objective

This week, we are going to review how we prepare the business for future opportunities and challenges. To start with, you need to be following trends and have regular access to information about what is happening in your country, your region, and globally.

Action

Foresight is an essential part of the planning process, as it will enable your business to assess its vision with the future rather than the past in mind. Society is changing fast, which means that your strategy and plans will need almost constant adjustment.

One of the biggest challenges for an organisation wanting to introduce trend following is that there is actually too much choice. There are many suppliers that specialise in trend following, as well as numerous advertising agencies offering similar services. It is therefore vital that you agree on *one* trend-following tool to use for the whole company.

Once that tool is chosen, review and identify the most relevant trends for each business or service you offer. This will avoid duplication of efforts, facilitate exchanges within the business, and ensure everyone both speaks the same language and understands the trends and implications in the same way.

Examples

Among the most talked-about trends for business at the moment are the following:

- aging baby-boomers
- apps
- authenticity
- crowdsourcing, innovative co-creation
- health and well-being
- heritage, nostalgia, tradition
- making the world a better place
- personalisation, individualisation
- showrooming
- subscriptions for all
- sustainability
- urbanisation

These are just a few of the many trends that suppliers are talking about these days. Instead of following them all, find which trends are the most relevant for your business or category and concentrate on watching their development.

Week 16: Review NPD Roll-out Plans

❝ *I don't set trends. I just find out what they are and exploit them*

Dick Clark, American radio and TV personality and cultural icon

Objective

Once you have identified the most important trends to follow, you need to identify their stage of development in each country or relevant market for every new product or service you plan to launch.

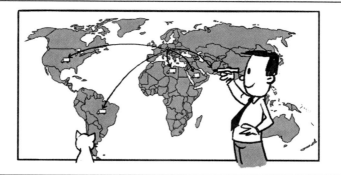

Action

Last week you identified the trends of most relevance for your product or service. This week, you need to plan how you will evaluate their development stage in each of your markets by running a relevant measurement study. This study will result in a ranking of the markets on each trend.

Next, identify the most relevant markets for the new product you plan to launch and ensure that the markets are prioritised for roll-out in the same order as their trend development. You may also identify some markets where the launch of the product is unlikely to meet with success, since the sensitivities of the customers are not sufficiently developed. In these cases, it would be best to delay the launch.

Examples

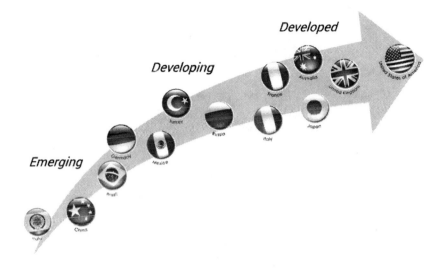

The above example shows how you can represent the positions of markets on a trend to show which are emerging, developing, and developed. This helps everyone to visualise the current situation. It allows markets to see which countries are ahead of them and from which they can learn what to expect. It also enables them to see which markets are behind them and to which they can provide support by sharing relevant experiences. Illustrating market development on each trend as shown above provides invaluable visual clues to a successful NPD roll-out plan.

Idea

If you plan the launches of each future new product and service in this way, and not merely by geographical proximity as most companies do, you are likely to meet with a significantly higher success rate.

Week 17: Develop Competitive Advantage

> **❝** *If you want one year of prosperity, grow grain.*
> *If you want ten years of prosperity, grow trees. If you*
> *want one hundred years of prosperity, grow people*
>
> **Chinese Proverb**

Objective

Now that the organisation is following one set of trends, it's time to take your foresight to the next level by transforming them into plausible future scenarios. It is scenarios and not trend-following that will enable you to get ahead of the competition.

Action

There is no competitive advantage in following societal trends, as everyone else is doing the same and often using exactly the same suppliers. You are therefore extremely likely to develop the same types of innovation as your competitors, and as a result, you're unlikely to meet with the success you expect. However, you can get an edge over the competition by developing trends into future scenarios and then identifying their trigger points.

Scenario-planning can often be done with the same organisation you are using to follow your trends, but it is of course a proprietary exercise and thus will cost you the same, if not even more, than your trend following. If you prefer to work with a specialist in scenario planning (which is highly recommended), C^3Centricity has developed a close partnership with one of the most uniquely creative suppliers in the world today, SciFutures, which uses science fiction for inspiration. Find out more about their exceptional Sci-Fi storytelling at http://SciFutures.com.

Whichever agency you use, they will usually develop your scenarios into appealing stories that can be visualised as presentations, animations, audios, and/or videos. These multiple dimensions will ensure the message gets shared in the most inspiring and actionable way across the whole organisation. As it is this second step that delivers true competitive advantage, it is definitely worth the extra investment. Scenarios are a strategic planning method that enables you to make flexible long-term plans and also be better prepared for the most likely future opportunities and challenges.

Most scenario work is done by extending the trends into the future and then combining them, to see how they impact one another and also your business. Two to three axes are then identified, referred to as the *axes of uncertainty*, on which the most extreme changes will occur and the corresponding "new worlds" described. The last part of the exercise is to position your categories and markets on the trends and to identify trigger points that will enable you to be forewarned of possible market changes.

Examples

The simple chart on the right shows four possible futures for customer centricity (CC) in a company. The two axes are the organisation's openness to change and whether or not they are ready to put the customer at the heart of their business.

As the scenarios show, only those ready and open to change will succeed in becoming customer centric. The other worlds will be less successful. Where are you today?

Week 18: Start Strategy Development

Objective

You have developed your vision and have ideas about what the future may hold for your business and brands. It is now time to take a look at the strategy you need to get there.

Action

In order to become more customer centric, it is a good idea to first review what you are currently doing in this area and identify any possible issues or opportunities that need to be addressed. Since the whole company should be involved in driving customer centricity by now, each department should run this review to see what they can do to help the whole organisation move forward. Everyone's objectives should include direct and frequent contact with customers and clear targets for these connections. Refer back to Week 7 for ideas on possible opportunities to connect.

Examples

Here are some examples gathered from different industries that will be useful when looking to improve customer centricity:

- Get your R & D group to invite customers to review and critique their new product ideas and concepts.
- Obtain customer input to your communication ideas, perhaps online.
- Ask all customers who call in or write to your care centre to provide an answer to one question. This could be the one thing they love or hate about your product, packaging, or advertising, or one new product that they would love you to make.
- Encourage your field representatives – sales reps, merchandisers, promoters, samplers – to regularly share what they have learned from interacting with customers this week and month.
- Request a review by your advertising and market research agencies of all they have learned about your category or brand – or the competition and their customers – in the last quarter, semester, or year.

Any of these will improve your customer centricity. Doing them all will put you well on your journey to becoming truly customer centric.

Idea

A final suggestion is to use the C³C Evaluator tool, which you can find at http://www.C3Centricity.com/C3CMembers. It provides your organisation with an accurate picture of where you are today in terms of customer centricity, as well as identify the actions you need to take to improve.

The C³C Evaluator can also be completed at regular intervals to measure your progress. Why not get people from each department, if not everyone in the organisation, to complete it for a comprehensive review of the organisation?

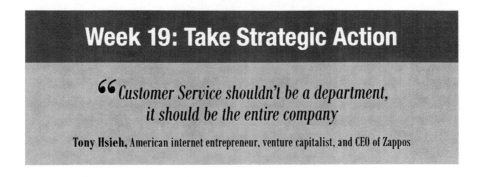

Week 19: Take Strategic Action

> **"** *Customer Service shouldn't be a department,*
> *it should be the entire company*
>
> **Tony Hsieh,** American internet entrepreneur, venture capitalist, and CEO of Zappos

Objective

Last week, you reviewed what you are currently doing in each department to put the customer at the heart of the business. This week, you need to agree on the improvements each department will make going forward.

Action

Once you know precisely from where you are starting, you can more easily decide what needs to change and then prioritize and plan these changes. Changes in what people think and feel is happening faster and faster, due in part to technological advances and improved global connectivity. It therefore makes sense to consider using shorter time frames when developing your detailed action plans, say three to six months at a time.

Most plans work on an annual or biannual basis. Whilst this can remain, they need to be broken down into smaller time frames when it comes to the actions to be taken. This then makes it easier to adjust during the life of the plan.

Examples

This week is all about assessing the customer-centric nature of your business plans and identifying needed changes. Here are some suggested actions that may help you start:

- Review your annual business plans and add a midterm review of your customer centricity, with expected results to be achieved by that time. A six-month time period is a good place to start in this rapidly changing world.
- Review departmental plans and confirm that your customers are mentioned as well as the impact the department's actions will have on their satisfaction.
- Review the customer connections achieved by each employee and make sure sharing sessions are taking place on a regular basis.

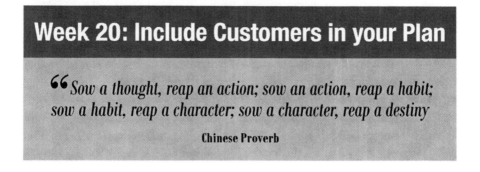

Week 20: Include Customers in your Plan

> 66 *Sow a thought, reap an action; sow an action, reap a habit; sow a habit, reap a character; sow a character, reap a destiny*
>
> **Chinese Proverb**

Objective

You have now identified how customer centric you are and the necessary actions needed to improve the way the customer is integrated into everything you do. This week, it is time to review the content of your business plan.

Action

Each business plan should include a detailed section on what actions you are planning to undertake in what time frame. A customer-centric company will consider how these activities are likely to be welcomed by the customer and how they will impact customers' opinion of each brand and the company as a whole. For organisations whose name is directly linked to the brand name, this becomes even more crucial.

Today's customer is also interested in learning about the company behind the brand, as well having access to information about the products or services they consume. Production resources used, sustainability, ecology, and origin are all important details that should be shared with today's savvy customer. By taking the customers' need for information into consideration before you develop your business plan, you will be able to identify any weaker areas which can then be addressed before you implement your plan.

Examples

Information to be considered for inclusion on product packaging:

- complete contact details for customers to connect using their preferred means (telephone numbers, website address, email, postal and street addresses)
- full ingredients list, including the sources of major ones
- suggested uses or warnings about usage

Information to be considered for inclusion on advertising:

- parent company identification, name, and logo
- QR code linking to website or other information sources
- website address for more information, online ordering options, or how to find local retail locations

Your Summary Results for the Company Section

Over the past nine weeks, you have spent a lot of time thinking about your business and the relevance of the customer in it. Review the below table and ensure that you have completed each recommended action in the nine areas. Remember, you can download a copy of the template at http://www. C3Centricity.com/C3CMembers and mark, for each, whether or not it has been completed.

Week	Result	Completed? (Y/N)
12	Have you made the customer more visible in your offices and your day-to-day business meetings and processes?	
13	Have you identified who will represent the customer within the organisation?	
14	Is your customer specifically mentioned in your mission and vision statements?	
15	Have you identified relevant trends for each of your categories and started tracking them regularly?	
16	Do you use these trends to help define roll-out plans of your new products and services?	
17	Have you developed plausible future scenarios to prepare your business for possible opportunities and challenges?	

Week	Result	Completed? (Y/N)
18	Are you regularly involving customers in your strategy planning and development work?	
19	Do your business plans have sections on customers and their likely reactions to your planned actions?	
20	Are you providing multiple contact details and information sources for your customers to obtain the information they may request?	

How well did you do? Don't worry if you couldn't say "yes" to all questions; customer centricity is a journey, not a destination. Completing a copy of the above template will make it easier for you to plan for further improvements when you next return to this section.

Introduction to Products and Services

It's not surprising that this next section, lasting eighteen weeks, is the longest to complete, as we will be covering what your company offers its customers in terms of products and services. After more than four months looking at how you innovate, what your customers think about your different offers, and how you keep track of it all, you will make some of the most customer-centric changes in your organisation. Are you ready to get started?

Objective

This week we start the section on improving your product and service offerings by making them more customer centric. Most companies start their innovation process by considering their strengths in technology or their current skills. Whilst this approach may work for renovations, breakthrough innovation often needs a different one. This is what we'll review this week.

Action

When you are looking to innovate, instead of starting with your internal technology and skills, or current products and services, how about taking a step back and thinking about what business you are really in? Lego is a great example of an organisation that did this and was able to turn around a declining business. The management understood that they were not selling (just) toys; they were in the imagination business. Which business are you in? Do you have an opportunity to redefine or expand it?

Examples

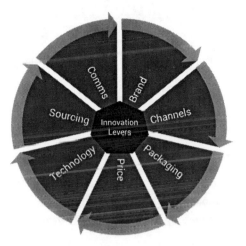

The above diagram shows a small selection of levers that can be used to expand your thinking when it comes to innovation. These same levers can also help you in redefining your business.

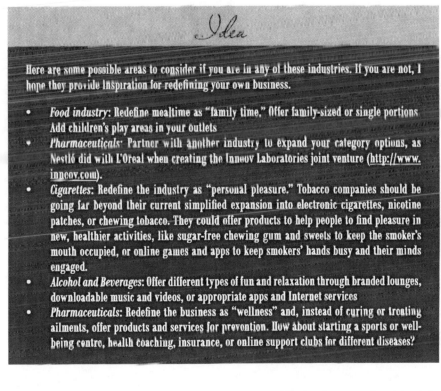

Idea

Here are some possible areas to consider if you are in any of these industries. If you are not, I hope they provide inspiration for redefining your own business.

- *Food industry:* Redefine mealtime as "family time." Offer family-sized or single portions. Add children's play areas in your outlets
- *Pharmaceuticals:* Partner with another industry to expand your category options, as Nestlé did with L'Oreal when creating the Innéov Laboratories joint venture (http://www.inneov.com).
- *Cigarettes:* Redefine the industry as "personal pleasure." Tobacco companies should be going far beyond their current simplified expansion into electronic cigarettes, nicotine patches, or chewing tobacco. They could offer products to help people to find pleasure in new, healthier activities, like sugar-free chewing gum and sweets to keep the smoker's mouth occupied, or online games and apps to keep smokers' hands busy and their minds engaged.
- *Alcohol and Beverages:* Offer different types of fun and relaxation through branded lounges, downloadable music and videos, or appropriate apps and Internet services
- *Pharmaceuticals:* Redefine the business as "wellness" and, instead of curing or treating ailments, offer products and services for prevention. How about starting a sports or well-being centre, health coaching, insurance, or online support clubs for different diseases?

Week 22: Review your Innovation Process

66 *Innovation distinguishes between a leader and a follower*

Steve Jobs, American entrepreneur and co-founder of Apple

Objective

Your products and services are only as good as the satisfaction they deliver to your customers. Humans are on a permanent quest for novelty and betterment and rarely stay satisfied for long, which is why innovation is a strategic essential for a successful business.

Action

Today's customers are highly demanding, because many of them have come to expect constant novelty and stimulation. As a result, innovation has become one of the most important ways to grow a business.

However, as Jan-Benedict Steenkamp – a marketing professor at UNC Kenan-Flagler University – proved a few years ago, successful innovation, at least for consumer packaged goods, is only achieved when the new product is positioned on one of the two extremes of "innovativeness":

- a minor improvement or renovation, such as a new flavour, size, colour, packaging, or content; or
- a radically new product that is significantly different from anything else on the market.

Radical new ideas are breakthroughs and usually more challenging to develop, but they are more likely to meet with success than smaller innovations. This is why many organisations look to launch renovations to keep current customers satisfied in their search for novelty, whilst developing true innovations which, although less frequent, will enable them to persuade many of their customers to upgrade and hopefully attract new customers as well.

Today's task is to review your current innovation pipeline and identify where each of your concepts is on the spectrum of innovativeness. From my experience, most companies' innovations tend to cluster in one part of the chart only. Do yours? Offers that land in the middle of the axis need to be either enhanced to make them radically new or simplified to become "just" renovations.

Examples

Past examples of breakthrough innovations have included microwave-ready meals, the Sony Walkman, the Nespresso coffee system, the iPhone, and now also the iPad and other tablets. Breakthrough innovation often comes from looking outside the box, even outside the company. Consider your customers in the totality of their daily lives and not just when they're using your product or service.

Looking outside the company may mean partnering with universities, which often have great ideas but lack the business knowledge to turn them into reality. Or how about creating a joint venture with a competitor in your industry that is lacking your skills but has complementary ones? The examples above should have inspired you to think wider in your innovations.

Week 23: Make R & D Customer Centric

"The real voyage of discovery consists not in
seeking new lands but seeing with new eyes

Marcel Proust, French novelist, critic, and essayist best known for his
monumental "À la recherche du temps perdu" — *In Search of Lost Time*)

Objective

Many companies develop new products and services based only upon their
current skills and technologies, which can be extremely limiting and not at all
customer centric. A better place to start would be by understanding customers
intimately and making offers that they need or desire.

Action

One way to help, if you believe you are faced with this problem, is to invite
your R & D (research and development) team members themselves to be
more customer centric. There are many ways to do this, but one of the fastest
is by introducing knowledge-sharing and insight development to them on a
regular basis. This can be done by incorporating an insight team into their
physical environment, or at least having part of the insight function working
exclusively or primarily with the developers and scientists.

My own experience with this suggests that R & D will very quickly become interested in seeing how potential customers react to new ideas long before they are precisely defined. The R & D team will understand that knowing their customers can add real value to their research and development, and they will end up getting more and more involved with market research projects, knowledge-sharing, and insight development.

Examples

Here are a few of the things I have found to work in raising R & D's interest in the customer:

- Encourage scientists to participate in a customer connection session; see Week 7 for more information about organising them.
- Share the latest news on customers on a regular basis – at least monthly.
- Circulate the latest suggestions and criticisms of your products and services that have been gathered by your care centres.
- Run co-creation sessions (more about those in Week 26).

Week 24: Reinvent your Innovation

> 66 *Creativity is thinking up new things. Innovation is doing new things*
>
> **Theodore Levitt,** American economist, professor at Harvard Business School, and editor of the Harvard Business Review

Objective

There are numerous ways to innovate, and many levers you can use, from business models to partnerships, as we saw in Week 21. One of the most effective ways to innovate in a way that builds emotional relationships with customers is through stimulating more of their senses. This week, you will review what you are currently offering and evaluate what you can add to make them more appealing to the senses.

The photo opposite shows how easy it is to add texture and design to a perhaps tasty, but still ordinary, cup of coffee. The design makes it a special occasion for the drinker and is a simple way to differentiate your offer.

Action

One way to successfully respond to customers' increasing demand for novelty is by adding sensory features to products and services. Your customers will become more attached to your offerings through the stimulation of multiple senses, which will have the added benefit of prompting further reasons to purchase and remain loyal.

Take each of your products and services in turn and evaluate what senses are already being stimulated, either by the item itself or by the way in which it is sold or communicated. When this evaluation has been completed, return to the list and see what might be added to make each item more multisensorial– whether by increasing a sensory element that is already present or by including additional ones.

Examples

These sensory additions from the current marketplace in several industries can give you some inspiration:

- New and even second-hand cars are impregnated with the smell of new leather, which appeals to buyers and makes them feel more comfortable when sitting in the vehicle.
- The "clunk" of a door, window, or bottle closing suggests solidity and security. The sound can even be used in advertising to suggest a higher quality than the product might otherwise be perceived to have. Opel's European ads (http://youtu.be/jv2TsNm1TBw) are a good example of this, demonstrating the German reputation for solid quality.
- Add surprising sensations to an ordinary product – for example, a chocolate coating on an individual ice-cream dessert that cracks when the spoon is dipped into it. The coating not only adds flavour but also texture and sound to the experience of eating.
- Add scratch-and-sniff stamps to the front of packs to attract buyers through smell.
- Add several colours within one product to suggest different ingredients or special benefits. Washing powders often use this form of differentiation, as does Dentyl mouthwash in the UK (http://www. dentylactive.com).
- A sound, musical jingle, or slogan added to the end of an advertisement can provide an additional attribute on which brand recall can be built. Purina's "Your pet, our passion" and music at the end of their commercials does both very well.

Week 25: Add Service to your Brand

Objective

Some products are actually designed to work with other items or services, which are quite often the more expensive part of the sales equation – for example, razors and blades, or espresso machines and their capsules. They also are usually brand-specific and in some cases can only be bought at certain outlets or even online. However, there are other brands that provide additional services to their customers, thus building upon their relationships and boosting loyalty, significantly in some cases.

Action

By now, you know a lot about your customers and their (maybe unmet) needs. Consider the environment in which they are using or consuming your product and see whether there are any opportunities to propose an additional service or a different but relevant product from your own portfolio. This may be just a sample of a current product or may involve the development of a completely new offering.

Examples

There are many organisations that are taking this route to satisfy and even surprise their customers, consumers, and clients:

- Starbucks offers more than coffee; the company's outlets are a "home away from home," with comfy sofas, free Internet, and tables for working and meetings. Starbucks even provides the possibility of listening to and purchasing music collections that are unique compilations played only in their stores.
- Purina sells pet insurance under the Purina Care brand, in association with Central States Indemnity Co. of Omaha.
- Gerber created its own Gerber Life Insurance Company and now offers a number of insurance plans, including the Gerber Life College Plan, a college savings and life-insurance plan; the Grow-Up Plan for children from fourteen days to fourteen years of age; and term life insurance for families.

What additional services can you offer your customers?

Week 26: Co-create your Innovations

> **❝** *I want to talk with people who care about things that matter that will make a life-changing difference*
>
> **Mark Victor Hansen,** American inspirational and motivational speaker, trainer, and author, best known as founder and co-creator of the *Chicken Soup for the Soul* book series

Objective

After having spent several weeks reviewing different ways to innovate, it is now time to change the actual process of innovating. This week we are going to start involving our customers directly in the development of our new concepts.

Action

Any company looking to become more customer centric should consider how it can incorporate customers' thoughts, ideas, needs, and desires into each product and service they offer. Co-creation has become popular in recent years, not only because of the ease of getting input directly from customers over the Internet, but also because it just makes good business sense.

A further advantage of the Web is that companies working regionally or globally can quickly gather information from different geographical areas in order to understand the similarities and differences between customers across the globe. This can help enormously when planning the roll-out of a new product.

This week, invite a group of your customers to join in a marketing plan or innovation meeting, to share their own ideas and to critique your current thinking.

Examples

Other ways to involve your customers in your innovation processes include the following:

- Ask customers who contact your care centres to mention one thing they would change in your product or service.
- Invite a group of customers to brainstorm ideas about possible future products and services to help you better understand their rational needs and emotional desires.
- Go shopping with your customers to better understand how choices are made and what elements of your offer could be improved.
- Set up an online panel of your customers and ask for their input on a regular basis. Procter & Gamble was one of the first to do this with their Tremor™ (for teens) and Vocalpoint™ (for mums) panels. Today many other organisations use them, including the following:
  - o Brewtopia (Australian) and Kaiser (Brazilian) beer brands invite consumers to vote on packaging
  - o BMW, Audi, and Boeing have developed virtual innovation labs which give car enthusiasts and aviation fans a say in product development.
  - o Converse, Cadillac, and Mercedes all use panels to help develop their advertising campaigns.
  - o Crayola drives demand with VIP Votes that let consumers decide on the names of new crayon colours.

Panels are hard work and costly to both set up and run successfully over the long term, but the rewards – not only in better product development but also the increased loyalty and advocacy that results – make them extremely attractive for most major companies.

> 66 *If we devote our time disparaging the products of our business rivals, we hurt business generally, reduce confidence, and increase discontent*
>
> **Edward N. Hurley,** chairman of the US Shipping Board during World War I

Objective

We are going to finish our coverage of innovation this week with a short review of product testing. It is an essential part of the process of measuring customer satisfaction and ensures that new products not only meet our customers' desires and needs but also perform at least as well as, and hopefully better than, our competitors'.

Action

Product testing is an essential on-going necessity for all companies. To stay current with both our own performance and that of our competitors, our products should be tested at least once and ideally several times a year. When was the last time you tested yours?

There is much discussion about the merits of monadic (single product) and sequential monadic testing (a single product tested at a time, followed by one or more in rotation). If you don't have any information on your product's performance and that of your main competitors, sequential monadic will arguably provide more information more quickly. If, however, you do have that information, you might consider moving to monadic testing or increasing the frequency of testing, especially in more dynamic markets. The importance of regular measurement cannot be stressed highly enough.

Examples

Whilst monadic testing is simple to conduct, sequential monadic must ensure that all products tested are evenly distributed across the order of testing.

Two product test:

- A followed by B for half the sample
- B followed by A for the other half of the sample.

Both sub-samples should be evenly matched in terms of basic demographics, usage and media consumption habits.

Three product test:

- A followed by B and then C for one-sixth of the sample
- A followed by C and then B for one-sixth of the sample
- B followed by C and then A for one-sixth of the sample
- B followed by A and then C for one-sixth of the sample
- C followed by A and then B for one-sixth of the sample
- C followed by B and then A for one-sixth of the sample

This method is often referred to as a round-robin test. It ensures that each product is tested in each position, thus eliminating order bias (a tendency for the last product tested to be preferred more often).

Whichever method you use, the most important point is to test regularly both your own products and those of your competitors.

Week 28: Create Customer-Centric Packs

Objective

Having checked that our products are performing optimally, this week we're going to look at our packs. Packaging has many functions, including the protection of the product inside, brand recognition, and impact on-shelf – as well as enabling the customer to use it, of course. This week, you should review your packaging to ensure it meets all its functions adequately.

Action

Observe how your customers are using your product in their normal daily lives, as well as the products of your major competitors. Identify issues they have whilst shopping for or using it. Additionally, try and identify the ways in which all category customers compensate for packaging that is less than ideal for them and then add this extra benefit for a competitive advantage.

It is interesting to note that we don't always realise that we are compensating for suboptimal packaging. We become so used to manipulating it that we no longer consciously notice what we are doing, which is why observation is a far better source of understanding than questioning.

Examples

Some recent examples of how manufacturers have been able to improve their packaging to make the user experience even more positive:

- Adding a simple handle to a larger pack makes it easier for customers to carry; these can be found today on dog food and toilet paper, but surprisingly not on all cat food and kitchen towels.
- Repackaging a product into smaller or single-portion packs makes sense if this is how most of your customers are using it. One further advantage of offering these smaller sizes is that customers are usually willing to pay a premium for the added convenience.
- Single-portion packs may find a further use in emerging markets, where the price point is of particular importance for attracting potential new customers.
- Invert the way a tube stands for thick or creamy substances – as Heinz did for their ketchup or many toothpaste manufacturers did for some of their brands.

Observation is the best method for identifying improvements, and it can provide great input on how to improve the product itself. Whilst watching your customers use the pack, you can note if they are also adapting the product's usage — enhancing it with additional ingredients, for example, or using it for purposes other than the one for which it was developed. These can all be useful inputs for R & D.

Week 29: Stretch Brands across Categories

> ❝A brand for a company is like a reputation for a person. You earn reputation by trying to do hard things well
>
> **Jeff Bezos,** American entrepreneur and CEO of Amazon.com Inc.

Objective

If you have a strong brand with an excellent reputation, why not take advantage of it by launching a new product or service in an adjacent category? Not only will the brand already be known to consumers, but the new product or service will start with an image that would otherwise take time to develop. In turn, the new addition may also improve the current image of the brand.

Action

If you are already present in several categories and with several brands, it's obviously easier to add something new. However, even if you only have one brand, consider what adjacent or complementary categories could be of interest to your current customers. Since you already know your customers well, it's easier to start with them in mind than to go after a completely new segment, at least in the beginning. As your confidence grows in stretching your brand, you can start to consider new segments and users too.

Examples

Procter & Gamble has done this very successfully, following an initiative conducted more than ten years ago to reduce the number of brands. With a smaller portfolio of brands to manage, the company then looked at stretching them into adjacent categories. For example, they combined the sheeting action of Cascade and the water-filtering technology of PUR to create a spotless car-wash product under the Mr Clean brand, and used a Pantene base and new perfumes from their fragrance resources to propose a successful new "beauty" positioning for Head & Shoulders in Europe.

Nestlé has many examples of doing this too, including extending their La Laitière dessert and Kit Kat confectionery brands into ice cream. Unilever recently extended their Axe (Lynx in the UK) brand from deodorants into shampoo, and beyond that into hair-styling products for women.

Using the above examples for inspiration, take each of your brands and identify adjacent categories into which you could, in theory, extend. Then review possible new products and their target customers.

Week 30: Understand Brand Perceptions

> 66 *Perception is merely reality filtered through the prism of your soul*
>
> **Christopher A. Ray,** author

Objective

You should now have a good idea of what you want your brand to stand for in the hearts and minds of your customers. However, unless you measure their perceptions, you will not know whether you are succeeding in building the right image.

Action

It is very important to follow the progression of your brand's image, since everything that happens in the marketplace – whether due to your or your competitors' actions – will have an influence on how customers perceive the brand. More importantly, perception often declines ahead of a sales loss, so equity metrics can serve as a useful warning signal that something is going wrong. In most cases, they provide you with sufficient time to take appropriate action before sales start to decline.

Brand image should be measured at least every two to three years, but it can be done annually if there is a lot of change happening in the market. Images don't move as fast as marketers would like or often believe they do, so more frequent measurement than this is unlikely to show significant differences from previous ratings.

This week, select or review the attributes you will use to measure the image and personality of your brand. Identify any obsolete characteristics and replace them with more relevant ones covering the new sensitivities of the market. Make sure you have attributes that measure all three areas of an image:

- rational, functional benefits;
- subjective, emotional attributes; and
- relational, cultural, and social connections.

The image of your major competitors should also be followed, since comparative ratings are more useful and actionable. Comparison will also highlight your strengths and development opportunities, which you will consider next week. The other advantage of taking competitive measurements is that you can keep abreast of changes in their offers, which might not always be visible otherwise.

Examples

The list of attributes measured should include several from each of the categories mentioned above. For example:

- rational, functional benefits, such as good taste, melts in the mouth, wide range of flavours, washes whiter, longer-lasting perfume;
- subjective, emotional attributes, such as a trustworthy brand, modern, high quality;
- relational, cultural, or social connection, such as a Swiss brand, trendy, used by young people.

You may want to add further sections to cover supplementary information on brand personality, price perception, and value perception.

Reviewing and adjusting brand-equity measures is as important as keeping their comparability. Therefore, getting it right in the first place is worth the extra effort and will avoid numerous changes in future years, which can be difficult and frustrating to manage.

Week 31: Compare Brand Images

❝A house of brands is like a family; each needs a role and a relationship to others

Jeffrey Sinclair, brand strategist

Objective

Last week, you analysed the images of both your brand and its major competitors. This week, it's time to identify your strengths and the possible development opportunities found in those images. You also need to decide which you will prioritise and address now, and within which time frame.

Action

Compare the ratings of your own brand and those of your two or three major competitors. Ensure that your image is strong in the areas you have identified as part of your desired image. If this is not the case, then work at identifying how you can further support the desired attributes before making the comparative review versus your competitors.

Identify the areas where you are scoring well below the competition and select one or two on which to work. Any more than that, and both your resources and the impact on the image will be seriously diluted.

Examples

In the chart below, Brand A is compared to its two major competitors.

- Brand A: Innovative, good value for money, a wide range of flavours
- Brand B: Good-tasting and good value for money
- Brand C: Good-tasting, high-quality brand that consumers trust.

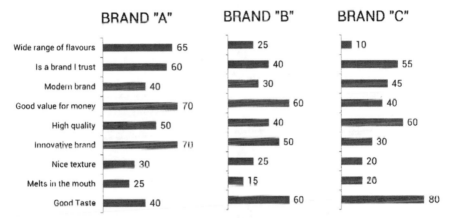

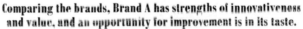

Comparing the brands, Brand A has strengths of innovativeness
and value, and an opportunity for improvement is in its taste.

Sometimes it is clearer to see the differences between brands when making a direct comparison as shown below. The individual scores for each brand are subtracted from one another, to highlight the major differences between them. The chart shows a simple percentage calculation, but indices can also be used.

Brands Compared	A and B	A and C
Wide range of flavours	40	55
Is a brand I trust	20	5
Modern brand	10	–5
Good value for money	10	30
High quality	10	–10
Innovative brand	20	40
Nice texture	5	10
Melts in the mouth	10	5
Good taste	–20	–40

The above table highlights that although Brand A scores well on value and innovativeness, its wide range of flavours is what really distinguishes it from its competition.

Week 32: Move Customers up the Funnel

"The journey of a thousand miles begins with a single step

Chinese Proverb

Objective

This week, you need to identify the differences in image that your brand has amongst its customers who are at different stages of experience. By doing this, you will gather information on which areas you need to correct and communicate to encourage customers to move up the levels.

Action

You are probably working with a path to purchase that resembles the one on the left of the opposite page. This is based on work done in 1898 by E. St. Elmo Lewis and was known then as the AIDA funnel model. In today's more complex world, the purchaser's journey shown on the right is becoming more common. Whilst the first can be of value, if the sample size of your image data permits, the one on the right will provide even greater granularity for your analysis.

Rework you image data by experience stage and then compare the differences. Keep in mind that your path to purchase may be more complicated than the simple one you are currently working with. Identify the strengths and development opportunities of both your brands and those of your competitors, and then plan appropriate actions and communications to build on your strengths and correct your weaknesses.

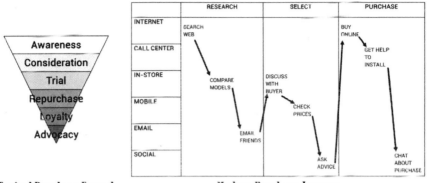

Typical Purchase Funnel   Modern Purchase Journey

Examples

The chart below shows a simple funnel analysis of brand images by level.

IMAGE OF BRAND "A" BY PURCHASE FUNNEL STAGE

Attributes	Total Image	Advocate	Loyal	Repurchase	Tried	Consider	Aware	Unaware
Wide range of flavours	65	90	75	75	70	60	60	20
Is a brand I trust	60	70	70	75	60	40	45	10
Modern brand	40	60	55	40	45	40	30	40
Good value for money	70	90	80	75	70	75	60	35
High quality	50	65	65	50	55	50	40	20
Innovative brand	70	85	85	70	70	60	40	20
Nice texture	30	35	40	40	35	20	20	10
Melts in the mouth	25	25	30	30	30	15	10	10
Good taste	40	55	40	45	40	15	10	10

Using the data for Brand A from last week's example, it can be seen that:

- reasons for considering Brand A are its innovative reputation and value (differences between consider and aware columns); and
- reasons for becoming an advocate and not just loyal to the brand are that it is perceived to be good-tasting with a wide range of flavours.

Of course, the overall image of being an innovative brand that is worth its price should not be forgotten – that received the highest overall scores.

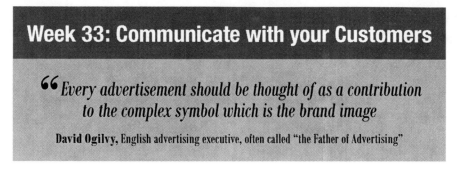

Week 33: Communicate with your Customers

❝ *Every advertisement should be thought of as a contribution to the complex symbol which is the brand image*

David Ogilvy, English advertising executive, often called "the Father of Advertising"

Objective

Now that you know which parts of your image need reinforcing or amending, it's time to ensure that all your communications are helping to improve your image and move it in the desired direction.

Action

Review the media habits of your target customers, as well as those of the subgroup that you need to influence. Plan changes where necessary. Make a complete list of all communications and the desired message of each. Compare these to the changes that are needed and decide on a clear action plan to make the adjustments as swiftly as possible.

The longer you continue to communicate on elements that do not take your image in the needed direction, the harder it will be to change your customers' opinion.

Examples

Continuing the example from last week, assuming we want to increase the trial of Brand A, we see that we need to increase the awareness of its excellent taste and texture. We could perhaps do this by emphasising these in communications, but sampling would be an even better solution, since those that have tried the product, score it much higher on these attributes. In addition, they score it lower on trust, something else that sampling should improve.

IMAGE OF BRAND "A" BY PURCHASE FUNNEL STAGE

Attributes	Total Image	Advocate	Loyal	Repurchase	Tried	Consider	Aware	Unaware
Wide range of flavours	65	90	75	75	70	60	60	20
Is a brand I trust	60	70	70	75	60	40	45	40
Modern brand	40	60	55	40	45	40	30	40
Good value for money	70	90	80	75	70	75	60	35
High quality	50	65	65	50	55	50	40	20
Innovative brand	70	85	85	70	70	60	40	20
Nice texture	30	35	40	40	35	20	20	20
Melts in the mouth	25	25	30	30	30	15	10	10
Good taste	40	55	40	45	40	15	10	10

Your communications partners will welcome the clear briefing that will result from the image changes needed for your brand and are much more likely to deliver work in line with your desired amendments: a win for you both!

Week 34: Measure your Company Image

Objective

You have already reviewed you brand-image metrics, revised them where necessary, and analysed them versus the competition and by funnel stage. You have also identified communication plans to correct and improve your brand image. This week, you will do a similar review for your company brand, particularly if it is not the same as your product but appears on packaging or advertising.

Action

Many organisations underestimate the importance of company image, especially when it is used in association with brands. If you are mentioning the name of your company on packaging or in communications, or perhaps it even appears as the brand name or part of it, then you must measure the perceptions of your company as well as that of the brand.

Once the company image has been evaluated, as is the case for any brand, it is important to plan communications to either support a desired positioning or to otherwise correct it. In addition, it should not be forgotten that a lack of customer centricity can have a negative impact on the trust and image of a company, as for example with repeated product-development failures.

This week, review both your company image and the link between your name and that of each of your brands. Evaluate what each brings to the other as well as whether there would be an advantage in using your company strengths more visibly in association with some or all of your brands.

Examples

Below are ways some companies have used their company name to support their brands:

- Add the company name more prominently on packaging.
- Include the company name and/or slogan at the end of commercials.
- Introduce innovations as coming from the company, especially if you know that it has a good image for creativity.
- Engage in multi-brand advertising and promotions under the umbrella of the company name.

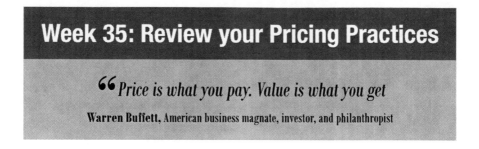

66 *Price is what you pay. Value is what you get*

Warren Buffett, American business magnate, investor, and philanthropist

Objective

Are you pricing your brand by merely adding a percentage to the cost of producing it? If so, then you could be missing out on additional sales and/or profit. This week, you will consider what your current, past, and potential customers appreciate about the value they are or will be getting and the estimated price they place on your offer.

Action

Review current pricing levels of both your brand and other brands in the category. Review also the results of your image measurement, if price and/or value attributes were included. If you believe pricing could be an issue for you – whether you believe your brand is overpriced or under-priced – then conduct a more detailed pricing study.

There are numerous ways of measuring value, the van Westendorp PSM (price-sensitivity methodology) being just one of them. Whatever measurement tool you use, make sure you will also be able to identify the psychological price barriers for your category and your brand, as well as for your competitors' brands.

If you find that your competitor is perceived to be offering better value for money, consider what additional benefits you can offer to increase the value perception of your own brand. Remember, it doesn't need to *cost* the actual increase in value perceived by the category users, but it should be something that your customers will appreciate and see as an additional benefit.

Examples

Here are some examples of improvements made to products to provide an increased value perception for customers. These all gave the manufacturers the ability to charge more – sometimes considerably more – than competitors for the same basic product quality.

- *Chocolate*: innovative packaging, appropriate for gifting or individual serving
- *Shampoo*: highly appealing new perfume
- *Coffee*: online purchase opportunity
- *Car Insurance*: 24/7 helpline
- *Hotels*: free Wi-Fi in room or free breakfast for executive-room guests
- *Airlines*: business-class check-in for premium economy travellers

Week 36: Quantify Brand Progress

Objective

Now that you have identified who you are targeting, the strategy to do so, and the desired image of the brand you want to develop, it is time to identify how you will measure your performance and growth.

Action

For each of your brands or services, your business plan includes a clear description of who you are targeting, as well as what actions you are going to take in the forthcoming period. Measurement of how well you are doing against the plan is essential and should include metrics beyond the basics of sales and profit. I know many companies who rely on sales and look to grow them by 5%, 10%, or more, and success is measured by achieving these set levels. What is wrong with that you might ask? A lot!

Suppose you are in a category or market that is growing at 50%, 100%, or more, as is the case in many industries in the developing countries of the world. This 5% or 10% growth now looks pretty feeble, doesn't it? In fact, if you grew sales above the target set in the plan – at say 20% – it would still mean you were losing share. So you need to add market share to your metrics.

This week, go back through your business plan and identify the metrics that are essential for you to follow in order to manage your business. Too much information and its impact is diluted; too little and you may miss valuable indicators.

Examples

Depending upon your industry, there are numerous customer metrics that can be followed. Here are just a few to get you thinking more about it.

For consumer goods:

- market size, market value
- market share, category share
- distribution, stock levels, out-of-stock
- brand image, brand equity
- price, perceived value

For lodging:

- occupancy
- social-media review scores
- revenue per available room (RevPAR)
- average daily rate (ADR)

For airlines:

- load factor
- available seat-miles (ASM)
- revenue passenger miles (RPM)
- fuel costs
- yield

Week 37: Evaluate your Performance

❝ *In business, words are words, explanations are explanations, promises are promises, but only performance is reality*

Harold S. Geneen, president of the ITT Corporation

Objective

Last week, you reviewed all the possible metrics you could use to follow the performance of your brand. This week, you will need to make tough decisions on which, out of all of them, are the most relevant. These will be your KPIs, or key performance indicators. You also need to consider measuring global company metrics, which will help you to follow your organisation's performance, as well as that of each of your brands.

Action

We have already seen the importance of following market share in addition to sales and profit. Another set of metrics all companies should follow, as mentioned in Week 30, is brand image and equity. These are like early warning signals when something is going wrong, since they usually weaken long before sales start to stagnate or decline.

Whereas it is important for a brand to have detailed information, at company level these metrics need to be summarised into just a few KPIs, through indexing or combining them. In addition to these brand KPIs, the organisation needs some other metrics that are important for the corporation and industry. See the examples below for some suggestions.

Examples

Corporate metrics should be kept to a minimum in order for management to be able to make a quick assessment of the health of the company. For example, brand image can be summarised as a one-number comparative index. Market share can be given globally or as an average for a region. The KPI can then become the share change or the number of markets, segments, or regions in which it is growing or declining. Price levels can be compared to average wage, the infamous "Big Mac" index, or something similar.

In addition to the business metrics, the following additional measurements may be needed for certain industries or company missions:

- safety, health, and environment for energy and mining industries
- employee satisfaction and engagement
- performance metrics such as deal closing or conversion rates
- impact of policies in the government sector
- competitiveness indices compared to competitive set
- innovation rate or rate versus plan
- stocks and inventories, especially in emerging markets.

> 66 *What gets measured, gets managed*

Peter F. Drucker, Austrian-born American management consultant, educator, and author

Objective

This week, one final thought on metrics concerns how you measure and compare them both internally and externally.

Action

Agreement on the most important metrics to follow for your own organisation and brands should be the result of internal discussions. Alignment of all departments and businesses on both the metrics themselves and the way in which they are to be measured is vital to the overall success of the exercise.

Also, the method used for gathering the information must be valid for each business, category, and market if they are to be compared. If they are not comparable, then proprietary metrics can be defined for each. However, as management should have a holistic view of the company's performance, the key metrics or KPIs should ideally use the same collection method wherever possible.

Both internal and external sources can be used to gather information about the business and then reduced to a few KPIs, as mentioned last week. These metrics should include comparisons to the performance of all major competitors, which also needs to be identified and agreed on for each business and category.

The advantage of developing company-wide metrics and KPIs is that comparisons can be made across brands, businesses, and regions, and then summarized in dashboards. These dashboards should be visual as much as possible, with colour coding and graphical rather than tabular results, so that the health of the business can be quickly ascertained.

Examples

Definitions that should be agreed upon across all business units of the organisation include:

- *Market share*, for which a minimum coverage level must be agreed upon for retail audit data to be accepted
- *Brand image*, a minimum of five to ten attributes that are the same across all brands within or across categories for comparability
- *Pricing*, the average price paid from retail audit measurement or willingness to pay from a brand equity or price sensitivity study
- *Purchase intention*, the top box or top two boxes from an identical three, five, seven, or ten-point scale.

Your Summary Results for the Products and Services Section

You've spent the last eighteen weeks reviewing everything you offer your customers and what they think about those offerings. Now is a great time to examine all the different topics covered, as you did with the last two sections, to ensure that you have completed every recommended action. Remember, you can download a copy of the template at http://www.C3Centricity.com/C3CMembers and mark, for each area, whether or not it has been completed.

Week	Results	Completed? (Y / N)
21	Have you redefined your business to provide an expanded view of innovation possibilities?	
22	Have you identified where each of your innovations is in terms of newness?	
23	Is your R & D department more customer centric and not developing new products and services based upon current technical skills and knowledge alone?	
24	Have you expanded your innovations by using more of the available levers?	
25	Has your increased knowledge about your customers enabled you to offer a new service or additional product offering?	

Week	Results	Completed? (Y / N)
26	Are your customers now a regular member of your innovation team for ideation and concept screening meetings?	
27	Have you introduced or increased regular product screening for both your own offers as well as those of your major competitors?	
28	Does your packaging now reflect a more customer-centric approach with relevant improvements that they value?	
29	Are your brands now competing in other relevant categories than those in which they were first launched?	
30	Do you know what your brand offers in terms of value across the three pillars of rational, emotional, and cultural benefits?	
31	Have you reviewed and started regular tracking of appropriate brand image and personality attributes for all your major brands?	
32	Are you analysing your brand-image scores by funnel stage to ensure customers are moving steadily towards purchase?	
33	Is your communication based on desired perception support or changes you have identified?	
34	Especially if different from your brand name, are you also measuring perceptions of your company image?	
35	Are your pricing practices based on value rather than cost alone?	
36	Do your plans include relevant metrics to cover desired progress in all relevant areas?	

Week	Results	Completed? (Y / N)
37	Have you selected appropriate KPIs (key performance indicators) to measure desired change and growth in the company?	
38	Are you comparing your metrics to those of your major competitors through equivalent measurements?	

How well did you do? Don't worry if you couldn't say yes to all questions; remember, customer centricity is a journey, not a destination. Completing a copy of the above template will make it easier for you to plan for further improvements when you next return to this section.

Introduction to Processes

In this final section, we'll cover how to bring together all the information and knowledge you have about your target customers, developing insights and sharing them across the organisation. These last three months will end with a review of the year, a new evaluation of where you are on your customer-centric journey, and the creation of a plan for the year ahead.

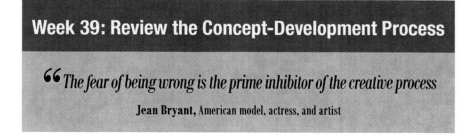

Week 39: Review the Concept-Development Process

> 66 *The fear of being wrong is the prime inhibitor of the creative process*
>
> **Jean Bryant,** American model, actress, and artist

Objective

Having reviewed who you're targeting and how your company structure, products, and services can be made more customer centric, it's time to review all the processes you are currently using. As the quote says, do not fear being wrong – only fear being wrong after launch if you did not ask your customers to join in the process.

Action

Almost all organisations create their own planning process for brand development. This week, take a look at your own process and see where you can make it more customer centric. Invite your customers to participate in the process at every stage.

A simplified example of the integrated planning process from a typical consumer-products company goes something like this:

1. Ideation
2. Conceptualisation
3. Industrialisation
4. Launch
5. Post-launch assessment.

Yours is probably very similar. Use the examples below to see how you can adapt your own process to include your customer in more of these steps.

Examples

Ideation:
- Review care centre records and social-media posts for customer comments about your current offers or those of your competitors.
- Invite customers to join a cross-functional or planning meeting.
- Run ethnographic research or accompanied shopper / usage sessions.

Conceptualisation:
- Invite customers to critique early-stage ideas for products or services.
- Measure interest in concept ideas before their development to prioritise your efforts.

Industrialisation:
- Run a small test market before launch and interview early users for possible improvements before roll-out.
- Identify the best communication media by following your target customers' media habits.

Post-launch:
- Review care centre contacts about the new offer to make any necessary adaptations quickly.
- Track posts on social media that comment on the new launch.
- Invite early adopters to participate in a post-launch workshop to further fine-tune your offerings.

These are just a few ways to engage customers in your development process. Any concept-generation and product-definition process can benefit from regular customer input. Invite customers to comment on your own recent launches or new development initiatives this week.

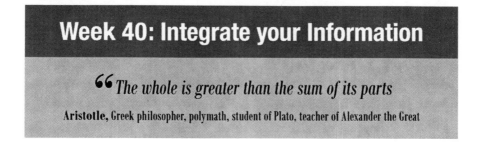

Week 40: Integrate your Information

❝The whole is greater than the sum of its parts

Aristotle, Greek philosopher, polymath, student of Plato, teacher of Alexander the Great

Objective

If your organisation is like most, you have a lot of information about your customers, but it's not all in one place or department. That's why we're going to take this week to prepare for the integration of all the knowledge and information available to you.

Action

We are lucky to be living in an information-rich environment where numerous data sources are readily available. However, this can also be a challenge, since we will need to identify the most relevant information sources for our business or industry from all of those we could use.

As you have now identified the most relevant information needed to follow your business, it's important to review the sources of that information and eliminate any duplication. As you review who has which piece of the puzzle, you may find that several departments have been buying the same reports or data. By cancelling all but one purchase, you will be saving money as well as encouraging the departments to work more closely together, since they probably all need different parts of the data.

One last recommendation is to identify who will be responsible for keeping regular contact with the supplier – negotiating contracts and circulating the needed information to each department.

Examples

There are many sources of information that different departments may need, with varying levels of complexity. I suggest you involve all departments in making a complete list of external information sources this week. In this way, nothing is forgotten, and everyone becomes aware of what is available within the organisation. Your list might include:

- market-share information from such companies as Nielsen, IRI, Canadean, and Millenium
- economic data from local governments, OECD, IMF, and NBER
- societal trend reports from specialised suppliers or advertising agencies
- financial and competitive analyses
- industry reports from relevant associations
- category or behavioural market research studies from numerous market research suppliers.

Week 41: Prioritise Information Integration

66 *Knowledge is a process of piling up facts;*
wisdom lies in their simplification

Martin H. Fischer, Swiss-American biochemist, awarded the 1992 Nobel Prize in medicine

Objective

Most integration involves setting up some form of database, whether a simple Excel spreadsheet, an Access database, or a more sophisticated IT platform. Whichever one is right for you, a decision must be made as to who is responsible for its updating and who has access to it. Many organisations shy away from providing wide access to all the information they have gathered, but this must be done in order to take advantage of differing perspectives from all departments within the company.

There will always be a certain amount of risk in providing access to any information within a company. Knowing and understanding information needs helps you weigh them against any risks.

Action

One way to prioritise the information to be integrated is to start with the metrics that have been agreed as your business KPIs. It will not be possible to consolidate everything in one go, so start with the most important and most used metrics. In many cases, the most valuable integration comes from combining internal and external information, as in the below examples. Further information can be added in the future, so keep this needed expansion in mind and allow for growth when developing any platform to manage your current data-integration needs.

Examples

There are, of course, multiple ways to integrate different data and information. The chart shows a few of the simpler and more common data sets that can be easily integrated. Their integration will provide far more knowledge and understanding than might be gained from simple analysis of each individual data set on its own.

INTEGRATE THIS	WITH THAT
Sales	Market shares
Representative visits	Distribution and out-of-stock
Social media reviews	Hotel bookings
Brand image	Market shares
Product performance	Brand equity

Week 42: Develop an Executive Dashboard

Objective

Gathering information and integrating it is only useful if it is easy to access and understand. Knowing your KPIs and how to integrate information are the first two steps; now you need to ensure that the right information is shared with the right people in your organisation.

Action

Circulate the analysis of the information you have gathered and integrated to all interested parties within the organisation. Now that you have set up and are regularly analysing masses of information, perhaps even in multiple databases, the summary findings will be best delivered in a dashboard.

Think of this as the cockpit of the company, like the one in an aeroplane. In the latter case, the pilot regularly scans the instruments to ensure he is going in the right direction, at the right speed, and with the best fuel economy. In the business world, top management are the pilots, and their metrics are the KPIs you identified in Week 37.

At the highest level of the organisation, the dashboard should be just one screen or page. Further screens and pages with more details can be provided to business units, geographic regions, and specific departments when additional depth is required.

The dashboard should be graphical rather than tabular in form. If numbers are included, use colour-coding to help management make a more rapid appraisal. In most cases, the red, orange, and green traffic-light colours are universally understood and thus appropriate, but if you use them to highlight bad, medium, and good performance, then don't use them elsewhere on the page with different meanings.

Also, if you want to colour-code scales of multiple results – such as population, sales, and profits – use graded single colours or warm to cool shades that can be easily understood, even without referring to the index. Wherever possible, make your charts logical and intuitive.

Another requirement for quick scanning is larger font sizes; if you need to reduce the font size to fit everything onto one page, then re-evaluate what you are showing. Is everything *really* key? Keep it short and simple.

Examples

Below are some examples of what you might show on that first page or screen for top management to review on a weekly or monthly basis:

- sales versus forecast, by total, source, geography, segment
- distribution, out-of-stock, stock levels
- orders versus revenues, averages
- pipeline velocity, innovation stats
- campaign investment, recall
- customer opportunities, days to close
- production versus deliveries, returns
- complaints versus sales, care centre contacts.

Ask your own management which key metrics they want to see on their personal dashboard. Don't be too creative by adding more than that, unless they agree upfront.

Week 43: Revise your Insight Process

> **❝A point of view can be a dangerous luxury when substituted for insight and understanding**
>
> **Marshall McLuhan,** Canadian philosopher of communication theory

Objective

In order to fully capture the value of all the information and knowledge your organisation has gathered about your customers, you need to have an insight-development process. If you do not have one in place, this week you will start to design it; if you *do* have one, then you can review it in comparison to the suggestions below to see whether or not it needs any updating.

Action

Designing an insight-development process usually includes turning data and information into knowledge and understanding, from which insights can be developed. If actions are taken before the information is understood or the insights developed, there is a chance that they will not be successful or profitable in the long term. This week, review the stage at which most of your decision-making happens and, if you are jumping to decision-making too early in the process, adjust your process.

Examples

There are many keys to turning data and information into knowledge and understanding, and then into insights. Here are a few suggestions to stimulate your thinking:

- Define the changes in your customers' behaviour and attitudes that you would like to encourage.
- Identify moments in your customers' decision-making or purchase journey that you would like to impact and define how to do it.
- Look for repeated issues, complaints, facts, or observations that you can address to improve your customers' lifestyle.
- Find connections between facts and information that were never noticed before and see whether this new perception leads to understanding and insight.

Week 44: Expand Knowledge-Sharing

Objective

One way to reduce your investment in information gathering, whilst at the same time increasing its value, is to share the developed knowledge and insights within your organisation. This is what you need to start doing or do more of this week.

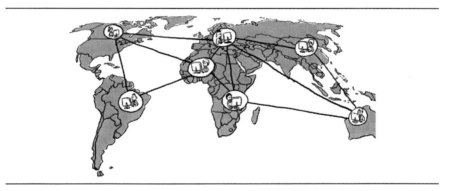

Action

Knowledge and insights within an organisation are usually held by the department or people who developed them. Increase sharing across the organisation and watch as customer understanding and insight development rapidly improve.

Examples

Sharing can be done in its simplest form by making summaries and circulating them on a regular basis. At its most complex (although not in terms of usage), an online database can be developed to manage all aspects of information gathering, analysing, reporting, and developing insights. If you decide to invest in a proprietary platform, the following are elements you may like to include. Add them to your summaries in the meantime, as a full online system will take months to complete.

- Store insights by customer segment and tag them by brand rather than the reverse; it is more customer centric.
- Summarise everything you have learnt in the last quarter or year about a specific segment of customers
- Insights coming out of one development exercise may be applied to other categories than the one for which they were originally identified.

Week 45: Prepare Interesting Presentations

> **❝** *To effectively communicate, we must realize that we are all different in the way we perceive the world and use this understanding as a guide to our communication with others*
>
> **Tony Robbins,** American self-help author and motivational speaker

Objective

As the above quote suggests, we all absorb information in different ways; some of us are visual, some auditory, and some are kinaesthetic learners. Keep this in mind when planning a presentation or knowledge-sharing session.

Action

Identify each team member's preferred way of communicating and then review a number of your past presentations. Adjust them as needed to include elements that will satisfy the main preferences of each adult learning type.

Examples

Visual: Think in pictures.

- Is the presentation only words and bullet points? Add an appropriate visual to each slide.
- Replace a table of numbers with a well-chosen graph.

Auditory: Tune in to sounds.

- Play a recorded discussion with your customer talking about your product or service, whether from your care centre or from market research interviews.
- Play or show competitive advertisements to compare with your own.

Kinaesthetic: Focus on feelings and physical sensations.

- Add an inspiring quote from an expert or celebrity to emphasise a point.
- Use storytelling to tune people in to their feelings, as stories create a visualisation in their minds.

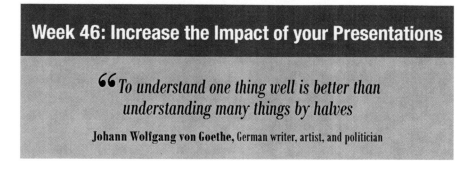

❝ *To understand one thing well is better than understanding many things by halves*

Johann Wolfgang von Goethe, German writer, artist, and politician

Objective

Having last week established the best style of content for presentations, this week we review what to include in it. As the above quote mentions, it is better to concentrate on making a few important points rather than trying to share everything you know or have found from your analyses.

Action

We all have too much to do and too much information to absorb. Help everyone by making your presentations shorter, so there is more discussion of the actions required, which otherwise might be limited or even left for a later meeting.

Concentrate on the three most important points you want to get across and the major information and understanding that led you to those decisions. Why three? Well, three is considered to be a *powerful number* by many cultures, and it is an ideal number when sharing or remembering ideas and concepts. Any further proof or knowledge can always be shared as an appendix or hand-out circulated before or after the presentation.

Examples

There are many ways to make presentations shorter and simpler, which everyone will appreciate. Here are a couple of techniques that both work very well and are easy to remember.

Presentations should follow one of two complementary C³Centricity rules, namely "10/20/30" or "3D – do, delegate, dump", depending upon whether you have a left or right-brain dominance.

For those who are left-brain dominant:

- Include __10__ slides that tell a compelling story
- Use __20__ words maximum per slide (and don't forget the pictures!).
- Keep to __30__ minutes maximum presentation length (to leave time for questions and discussion).

For those who are right-brain dominant:

- __DO__: Tell a story; don't show each project step completed or the results of each question asked in a market research project.
- __DELEGATE__: You have been chosen to give the presentation, so people have trusted you to have done a detailed analysis. You don't need to prove it by sharing every step or thought process you went through in coming to your recommendations. Participants will always ask for clarification when needed.
- __DUMP__: Dump all but the most relevant slides that cover your three most important points. Counting for introduction and conclusion slides, this means only two or three slides on each point. Ideally, group your findings and recommendations or discussion points into three topics.

Whichever rule you decide to follow, and they are complementary, your presentations will be more appreciated and your ideas better retained.

Week 47: Encourage more Storytelling

" *If you can't sum up the story in a sentence,*
you don't know what you're talking about

Garr Reynolds, American college professor, designer, musician, best-selling author

Objective

Storytelling has been used down through the ages to share knowledge in an appealing and memorable way. For this reason, it is a good idea to consider some best practices to incorporate storytelling into your own knowledge-sharing.

Action

Find inspiration by reviewing the contents of the websites mentioned in the examples section. Then define your own way of developing your information-sharing into more of a story. There are many free resources on the Web, and they can be grouped into five steps:

1. Gather the information you would like to share; include only the major details and numbers. See last week's comment about the power of three.
2. Choose a theme and structure for your story from amongst many major types. Themes may include evolution, crisis, opportunity,

crossroads, or dreams. Structures may be linear, situation/complexity/resolution, compare and contrast, or freeform (follow the audience).

3. Describe your customers in detail – not just who they are, but what they do and why. Remember the 4Ws from Week 5.

4. Explain the situation customers are in, their issues, and your opportunity, and build your argument around the theme and structure chosen.

5. Propose the solution – your recommendation – and make sure to share a happy ending.

Keeping to this five-step process will ensure that you include all major elements that will get your message across with little need for further explanation.

Examples

Review the contents of the following websites for inspiration:

- TED (http://www.ted.com) has as its motto "Ideas worth spreading." Most of these presentations get their messages across in less than twenty minutes. Those of Hans Rosling are particularly impressive for simplifying complex theories.
- Information is Beautiful (http://www.informationisbeautiful.net) from David McCandless (http://www.davidmccandless.com) includes some other great examples specifically for sharing complex data in graphical form.
- The Brand Stories website (http://www.brandstories.net) has a wonderful collection of stories on some of the best-known brands around. Read them for inspiration as well as for the useful examples, which are great for sharing.
- Garr Reynolds own website (http://www.garrreynolds.com) where he shares presentation tips and his blog (http://www.presentationzen.com) where he posts about issues in professional presentation design.

> 66 *Wise men profit more from fools than fools from wise men; for the wise men shun the mistakes of fools, but fools do not imitate the successes of the wise*
>
> **Cato the Elder (Marcus Porcius Cato)**, Roman statesman

Objective

The return on your investment in the collection of data and knowledge can be significantly increased by sharing. This week, look at your current sharing practices and identify how you can make your information more accessible to more people.

Action

Do you have a knowledge and insight library, accessible to almost everyone in the company? If so, there are ways to improve its interface to make it more user-friendly. Have a look at your platform and see what changes you can make.

If you are at a lower level of knowledge-sharing than this, then you will need to review what you have to share and the best way to do it. This could be a simple shared folder in Excel or Word, an Access database, an information library, or a full project-management system.

No matter what level you're at, I'm sure you can make some improvements to your current practices. And even before that, just informing everyone about what information is available internally would be a great first step. You should also define availability rules if you open access to a wider audience than in the past.

Examples

Sharing platforms can be as simple or as complex as you want. Here are some ideas on what to store and share, using readily available systems:

- *Excel* for the latest market research data or a summary of it
- *Word* for the latest reports or executive summaries
- *Access* to the latest reports, files, and folders, organised by category, brand, or customer segment
- *Library* for physical or online reports, both internal and external.

If you want to move to the next level and build a proprietary platform, take a look at the superb platforms designed by C³Centricity partner Insight Marketing Systems. Find out more about them at http://www.insightmarketing.com.au.

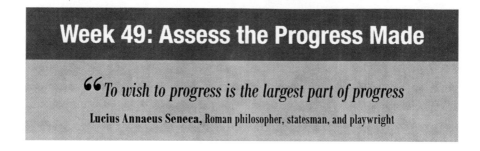

Week 49: Assess the Progress Made

> ❝ *To wish to progress is the largest part of progress*
>
> **Lucius Annaeus Seneca,** Roman philosopher, statesman, and playwright

Objective

As we approach the end of the year, these last few weeks will be review time. How far have you come, what have you achieved, and what still needs to be changed?

Action

If you have been following the weekly suggestions, then you will see that your business is far more customer centric than it was this time last year. It is now time to take a look at your current business categories and brands, and make a ruthless assessment of their long-term viability. With the large amount of information you now have available about each of your products/services and their customers, it is time to make some informed decisions for the coming year's activities.

Be firm about which categories you want to compete in and the brands you want to support in each. Identify those that you will stop selling or offer for acquisition, together with a clear timeline for doing so. Be ruthless in eliminating all those that do not fit into your current or future business plans.

Examples

It is always a tough decision to eliminate brands and products from your portfolio, but remember that others have successfully done it. With a streamlined list of brands to support, your marketing will be more focussed and your budget will be less stretched. Start with these suggestions:

- If you are like most companies, you will do 80% of your business from just 20% of your portfolio (Pareto's principle). Consider axing the bottom 5% to start with. Both Unilever and Procter & Gamble have reduced the number of their brands significantly in the last fifteen to twenty years and continue to do so from time to time.
- If you have several brands competing in one sub-segment but lack a brand in another, could one of them be repositioned?
- If you want to sell healthier food and beverage products, renovate or eliminate those with too much salt, sugar, or fat. Nestlé started doing this a few years ago as they redefined themselves as a health, wellness, and nutrition company.

Week 50: Re-evaluate your Customer Centricity

> **❝** We are very apt to measure ourselves by our aspiration instead of our performance. But in truth, the conduct of our lives is the only proof of the sincerity of our hearts
>
> **Anonymous**

Objective

This is the last week of your customer-centricity improvement year. It is time to review how far you have come and then plan what further changes are needed for the coming twelve months.

Action

If you completed the C³C Evaluator questionnaire at the beginning of the year, then it will be easy for you to measure how far you have come. The results will also provide you with a clear indication of what priorities you need to set to continue improving your customer centricity next year. However, if you have not completed the questionnaire, you should do it immediately so that your progress will be easier to ascertain next year. Go to http://www.C3Centricity.com/C3CMembers and complete it now.

Examples

Other ways to evaluate your progress in customer centricity and to prepare for the coming year might include the following:

- Review the results of the major KPIs you identified in the weeks on products and services.
- Identify processes that no longer meet your updated requirements. Perhaps you found some improvements that should be made when going through each week? If so, why not go back over your notes and identify which you will tackle in the next twelve months?
- Look back over your marketing plan and identify new or improved sections that will need to be included.
- Consider the objectives put in place for the customer connectedness of all employees. Were they sufficient to improve everyone's understanding of your customers? If not, they should be increased in length, type, or frequency.

Your Summary Results for the Processes Section

You have spent the last twelve weeks reviewing all the information you have, turning it into insights, and then sharing your knowledge across the organisation. Now is a great time to review all the recommended actions to ensure that you have completed them. Don't forget to download the template at http://www.C3Centricity.com/C3CMembers and mark whether or not each action has been completed.

Week	Results	Completed? (Y/N)
39	Have you made your planning process more customer centric?	
40	Have you identified the most relevant information sources and any cost-saving opportunities?	
41	Are you prioritising information-gathering and integration in line with your KPIs?	
42	Are you regularly reporting your KPIs to management in a summary dashboard?	
43	Have you developed a new insight-development process or revised your current one?	
44	Are you sharing more of your information and insights across the whole organisation?	

Week	Results	Completed? (Y/N)
45	Have you reviewed your presentation-development process and regularly incorporate visuals, sounds, and emotional stimulation into them?	
46	Are your presentations shorter and more focussed on three main points to communicate in a short, sharp way?	
47	Have you incorporated more storytelling into your presentations?	
48	Have you created a folder, database, or platform for sharing information and insights across the organisation?	
49	Have you reviewed the products and categories you are selling in relation to your new customer centric approach?	
50	Are you clear about the progress you've made in the past year and the areas that need attention and planning in the year ahead?	

How did you do? Don't worry if you couldn't say yes to every question. Remember, customer centricity is a journey, not a destination. Completing the above template will make it easier for you to plan further improvements when you next return to this section.

In Conclusion

Congratulations! You can be very proud of the changes you have made in your organisation over the past year. You have made a huge improvement to the customer centricity of your company, and I am sure your customers have noticed. Are you aware of just how far you have come?

In reviewing the KPIs you identified with which to manage your business, you will certainly find that some have significantly increased compared to last year, whilst others may have moved only slightly or not at all. Be proud of the changes you have made *1-Day* at a time. Many of them would not have happened without this book to support and guide you.

If you found the book useful, please let your friends and colleagues know. And if you see changes or improvements that would make it even better, let me know that too. I would love to hear from you.

In closing, I would like to encourage you to keep an eye on our website (www. C3Centricity. Com) for an announcement about the next 1-Day book, which I am currently writing. It is tentatively called Winning Actionable Insight and includes fifty steps to improved knowledge gathering, understanding and actionable insight development.

Can you think of other topics that you would be interested in having in this format? If so, please let me know; I might just dedicate it to you!

Attribution of Images

The majority of the wonderful illustrations in this book were expertly drawn by Agung Nurhidayat, alias StudioKimUS.

This book also uses pictures from many other sources, some requiring attribution, some not. However as a service to others who would like to use similar images, I provide the sources of them all.

Brozermo: Cover image
C³Centricity: Introduction, 4, 5, 16, 17, 21, 24, 31, 32, 41
Econsultancy: 3
Joost Beucken: 62

Legal Disclaimer

Every effort has been made to accurately represent this product and its potential, but there is no guarantee that you will become excellent in customer centricity using the techniques and ideas in this e-book. Actions, examples, and templates included are not to be interpreted as a promise or guarantee of success. Potential is entirely dependent upon the person using this fifty-step process and taking the actions detailed herein.

Your level of success in attaining the results suggested here depends upon the time and effort you devote to the actions, ideas, and techniques mentioned, as well as your own knowledge and skills in the different areas covered. Since these factors differ according to individuals, we cannot guarantee your success from following this fifty-step process. Nor are we responsible for any of your actions.

Materials in our product and our website may contain information that includes or is based upon forward-looking statements within the meaning of the Securities Litigation Reform Act of 1995. Forward-looking statements give our expectations or forecasts of future events. You can identify these statements by the fact that they do not relate strictly to historical or current facts. They use words such as "estimate," "expect," "intend," "plan," "believe," and other words and terms of similar meaning in connection with a description of potential earnings or financial performance.

Any and all forward-looking statements here or on any of our sales material are intended to express our opinion of earnings potential. Many factors will be important in determining your actual results and no guarantees are made that you will achieve results similar to ours or anybody else's – in fact no guarantees are made that you will achieve any results from our ideas and the techniques in our material.

Index

Symbols

A

B

C

D

E